RABBITS & SPAGHETTI

Captives and Comrades: Australians, Italians
and the War, 1939–1945.

talking History with
BILL BUNBURY

Many Australians fought and were captured in Italy
during the World War Two. A large number of these
POWs escaped, some to neutral Switzerland, whilst
others to join the Italian partisans in their struggle,
first against Mussolini's fascists and then the German
occupation forces. Most of these Australians depended
for their lives on the support and friendship of
ordinary Italian people.

Meanwhile, on the home front, Italian-born
Australians were taken from their families, their farms
and their businesses and interned in concentration
camps, and Italian soldiers captured in north Africa
were shipped to Australia where they provided much-
needed farm labour with the troops away at war. This
imprisonment in Australia was also relieved for many
by the compassion and goodwill of ordinary
Australians.

Bill Bunbury talks to men and women who lived
through these extraordinary, little known experiences.
They tell of the fear, hardship and despair, the courage
and the joys, and above all, of the wonderful friendships forged from adversity.

Rabbits and Spaghetti is based on Bill Bunbury's
popular ABC social history radio programs. It is a
lively, highly readable collection of historical snapshots,
in both words and photographs.

BILL BUNBURY is a producer with
the ABC's Social History Unit, and
is the presenter of 'That's History'
each Sunday on Radio National. His
books include *Reading Labels on Jam
Tins: Living Through Difficult Times*
(Fremantle Arts Centre Press, 1993),
*Rag Sticks and Wire. Australians In the
Air: Civil Aviation 1919-1980* (ABC
Books, 1993), *Cyclone Tracy: Picking
up the Pieces* (Fremantle Arts Centre
Press, 1994). He also co-wrote, with
Ros Bowden, *Being Aboriginal* (Allen
& Unwin, 1990)

Photograph courtesy ABC.

RABBITS & SPAGHETTI

CAPTIVES AND COMRADES
AUSTRALIANS, ITALIANS
AND THE WAR

1939–1945

talking history with
BILL BUNBURY

FREMANTLE ARTS CENTRE PRESS

First published 1995 by
FREMANTLE ARTS CENTRE PRESS
193 South Terrace (PO Box 320), South Fremantle
Western Australia 6162.

Picture Editor Helen Garwood.
Consultant Editor B R Coffey.
Designed by John Douglass.
Production Coordinator Linda Martin.

Typeset in Times by Fremantle Arts Centre Press and
printed on 115 gsm Silk Matt by Lamb Print, Perth, Western Australia.

National Library of Australia
Cataloguing-in-publication data

Bunbury, Bill.
    Rabbits and spaghetti.

    ISBN 1 86368 122 1.

    1. Prisoners of war — Italy. 2. Prisoners of war — Australia. 3. World War,
    1939-1945 — Prisoners and prisons, Italian. 4. World War, 1939-1945 —
    Prisoners and prisons, Australian. 5. World War, 1939-1945 — Concentration
    camps — Australia. 6. World War, 1939-1945 — Concentration camps — Italy.
    I. Title.

940.547245

Department for
theArts
Western Australia

The State of Western Australia has made an investment in this
project through the Department for the Arts.

This book is dedicated to the remarkable spirit of kindness and humanity, which, in the middle of one of history's worst wars, enabled so many men and women to see strangers not as the enemy but as fellow human beings.

ACKNOWLEDGEMENTS

There are always so many people to thank after writing any book. I'd like once again to thank my wife, Jenny, for her patient scrutiny of drafts at all stages of the book's progress. I'd also like to acknowledge the help of Lorraine Crook who undertook some of the early interviews with farming families who were hosts to Italian prisoners of war and, in the same context, John Kinder of the Department of Italian Studies, University of Western Australia, who also helped with both interviews and translations of POW interviewees. Historian Dino Gava of Edith Cowan University provided the original inspiration for the radio program on internment. Historians Roger Absalom, and Richard and Michal Bosworth also provided help and advice. My thanks also to Johanna Draffin for painstaking tape transcription. I'd like also to acknowledge the tellers of these stories, the Italian and Australian women and men who lived these experiences. They all have my grateful appreciation.

Finally I'd like to thank Publisher Ray Coffey, Photoresearcher Helen Garwood and Designer John Douglass of Fremantle Arts Centre Press for their considerable help and guidance in the production of this book.

Helen Garwood would like to acknowledge the help of the following in her search for visual material: Michal Bosworth; Anne Brake, Fremantle Prison; Prudence Broad; Josephine Cabassi and Loretta Baldassar; Lalage Falconer; Mary Fedele and Jo Rotondella; Rupert Gerritsen; Phil Loffman; Neville Marsh; Muriel McMahon; Yvonne Mouritz; John Peck; Lou Sgambelluri; the Varone family; and all the people who gave their personal photographs to Bill Bunbury.

CONTENTS

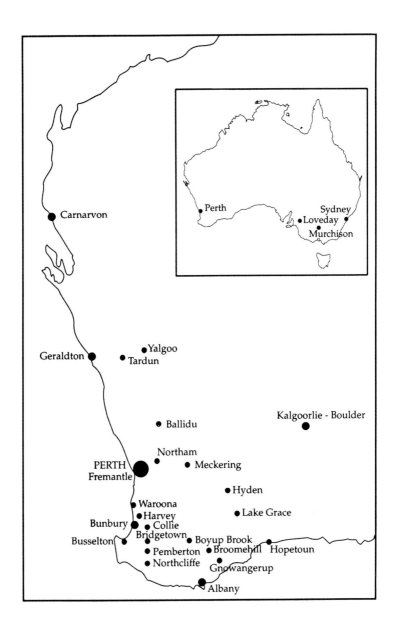

Carnarvon

Perth   Sydney
Loveday
Murchison

Yalgoo
Geraldton   Tardun

Kalgoorlie - Boulder

Ballidu

Northam
PERTH   Meckering
Fremantle

Hyden

Waroona
Harvey   Lake Grace
Bunbury   Collie
Bridgetown
Busselton   Boyup Brook
Pemberton   Broomehill   Hopetoun
Northcliffe
Gnowangerup
Albany

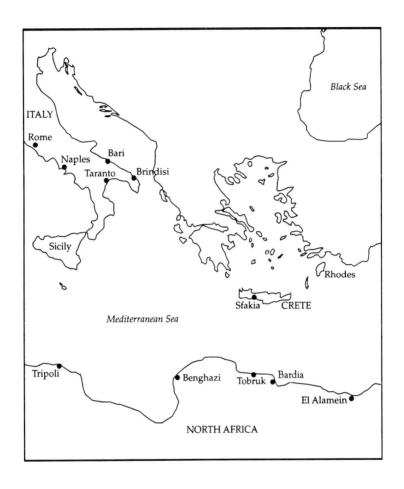

INTRODUCTION

The title *Rabbits and Spaghetti* came from a comment by an Italian POW to the effect that there were *milione de conigli* — millions of rabbits — on the Wheatbelt farm where he was sent to work in 1943. The other association — with spaghetti — came from the willingness of farmers' wives to let the POWs cook in their own way and often learn from them. The *milione de conigli* merged with the spaghetti in that most unifying aspect of human culture — food. The friendships that grew from those wartime meals are one of the major themes of this book.

Australian POWs taken to Italy did not always fare as well in the food stakes as their Italian counterparts in Australia, but they too learnt the value of friendship and often rewarded it in the difficult years 1943–45 when Italy was caught in the middle of the struggle between the Allied liberators and German forces determined to hold onto the peninsula.

Other contributors to this story are civilians, men and women who had left politics behind them in their native Italy and had come to Australia to find a new life in the 1930s. It was their misfortune to be caught in the middle of the European conflict, when Australia followed England into war against Italy in 1940.

The material for this book began with three ABC Radio National features on the experience of internment and imprisonment. However, listener response to these programs and further interviews and research encouraged me to follow the subject further. I've tried to retain the atmosphere of the original material and catch something of the intense, often dangerous but fully realised life of many men and women during the years 1939–1946.

Italian prisoners of war leaving compound for transport to the tomato gardens, Murchison Camp, Victoria.

PUT AWAY FOR THE DURATION
Italian Internment in Australia

I think Australia made some horrible blues on that side.
You know they were all homely people. All their children
were born here. Half of them were in the Army! Good
heavens! What were they going to do?

Joe Iannello, from Fremantle, private in the Citizen's
Military Force (CMF) in World War Two.

On 27 September 1940 Germany, Italy and Japan signed a mutual defence pact. Britain formally declared war on Italy, and Australia, taking a dutiful lead, followed suit. Italian settlers in Australia had, however, already paid a price for their country's political and military alignment with Nazi Germany. All over Australia, during June that year, following the rapid fall of France, Italians were rounded up and interned, regardless of how long they had lived in Australia. Many who thought of themselves as Australians now found they were potential suspects in their adopted land. They had left Italy but not Italian politics. For the next six years their lives would be affected by an international conflict that had little to do with them and their reasons for coming to Australia in the first place.

Benito Mussolini's fascist regime in Italy had predated Adolf Hitler's Third Reich, coming to power in 1922 and anticipating the Fuhrer's dream of lebensraum by its own imperial adventures in Ethiopia and elsewhere. Mussolini's internal reforms had given Italy the outward appearance of a modern superstate. Grandiose modern buildings in Rome could remind the citizens of the glories of their two-thousand-year-old empire. Mussolini drained marshes, increased agricultural production and (legendary cliché) the trains now ran on time. However, contradictions abounded within the country itself and deep political divisions remained. These would resurface with the outbreak of war with Britain.

However, in faraway Australia these concerns, for many Italian emigrants, were distant matters that scarcely concerned them. Many took pride in what Italy had achieved but for most there were more immediate concerns in prewar, post-depression Australia. Moreover, their interest in the fortunes of the Italian state depended on the region they had come from themselves. Italy had only become a united country almost within living memory. World War Two would test Italian unity in both a geographic and a political sense.

Internment would also pose a test for Australia's maturity as a tolerant nation. Many Italians, along other European nationals, had already made Australia their home well before World War Two and well before 'multiculturalism' became part of our vocabulary. The Commonwealth Government, acting under the provisions of the National Security Act of 1939-1940, could intern any person whose loyalty to Australia was suspect and who engaged in subversive activities. In practice, however, the Commonwealth delegated much of the detail to the military authorities and to state police forces, operating through their own governments.

This practice, it is now clear, resulted in more than the occasional case of unjustified internment. Subversive activities were vaguely defined, tending to equate loose talk with deliberate acts of disloyalty. Police forces could also be influenced by complaints from xenophobic citizens, who saw foreigners as threatening competitors.

The military for its part, tended to see 'alien threats' in strategic terms. If Italians lived in an area of Australia with a significant risk of invasion, they were more likely to be interned. Hence, in two States in particular, Queensland and Western Australia, both States with long, empty coastlines, the rate of internment was much higher than elsewhere and, in many cases, was influenced by local pressures quite as much as any concern for national security. Between them these two States interned two-thirds of

Fremantle, c.1940.

the almost five thousand Italians who went behind the wire 'in the national interest'.

Strategic considerations were, in the military view, quite genuine. The long unguarded coastlines of both Queensland and Western Australia presented a security risk in wartime. These lonely shores could provide opportunities for contact between invaders and a so-called fifth column. This 'treacherous band' might include anyone whose original loyalties could be seen as not towards the British Crown or the Australian way of life. However, despite an intensive and diligent search by the Commonwealth authorities from 1932 onwards, their agents were never able to identify any traitors.

In Queensland's far north, where individual Italians had been successful canecutters, growers and tobacco farmers, some soldier-settlers who had farmed the same land and failed, resented Italian rural enterprise and energy and were more than keen to see them interned. Some of the strongest expressions of hatred came from returned servicemen. They played up fear of 'the olive peril' and accused Italians of staying at home while 'our boys' were off fighting the enemy. In some coastal towns where larger numbers of Italians had lived alongside Anglo-Australians for a long time, there was often far more acceptance.

Internment in Western Australia, though not often carried out with the same degree of malice, was nevertheless heavy-handed and just as destructive in its effect. It also proved not to be in the national interest when Italians went to prison and wartime food production went down.

Without warning over a thousand Italian males were interned as enemy aliens and their families were left to cope as best they could. Imprisonment for many began in the chill of winter on Rottnest Island, where, in the previous century innumerable Aboriginal prisoners had lived out their last days far from their homelands. Some internees were sent to Fremantle gaol and all went later to the newly constructed internment camp at Harvey. Others, often members of the same families, while not interned, were manpowered and required to serve in the CMF. In 1942 the Civil Alien Corps was set up to absorb internees released from camps but not allowed back into their normal jobs. In the Corps they worked at road construction or in timber mills, under close military supervision.

Italian workers already reflected the diversity of the State's occupations. In the Eastern Goldfields many worked as wood gatherers, miners, shopkeepers or hoteliers. There had been tension between Italian and Anglo-Australian miners in Kalgoorlie-Boulder ever since World War One, culminating in the infamous riots of 1934. Much of the animosity was based on resentment of Italian productivity. Some of that feeling still lingered in 1940, and, in the Goldfields, helped swell the number of 'suspect aliens' reported to the authorities.

In the Fremantle area Italians were skilled tradesmen, fishermen, businessmen, tailors, barbers or shopkeepers. Their wives worked at home or in local factories. Others tilled market gardens north and south of Perth.

Further out, some had set up fruit and vegetable cooperatives in the Darling Ranges and in the stone-fruit district of Donnybrook in the South-West. Italians also made up a sizeable part of the agricultural workforce in the South-West. Many lived in and around Waroona and Harvey, rural production centres of vegetable and dairy products. Futher north, at the port of Geraldton, Italians also worked as market gardeners and fishermen.

In all these districts Italians were to either undergo internment themselves or be profoundly affected by the experience.

Frances Iannello, a distant cousin and, later, wife of Joe Iannello, was born in the picturesque port of Capo d'Orlando, not far from Sicily's capital, Messina. Frances and her family had come to Fremantle in 1931, when she was eleven years old. Her father spent four years at the front in World War One, when Italy had fought as an ally of Britain and France.

Like many men of his generation he was a ceaseless migrant,

earning his living as an engineer, travelling alternately to the United States, Australia, and, every five years or so, home to Sicily. Her mother brought up the children largely on her own. Frances saw her father for the first time when she was five, when he made a brief visit to Capo d'Orlando. The next time she saw him she was eleven and he was waiting for them on the wharf at Fremantle. His wandering days were over. He had a house ready for the family and their life in Australia began. However, these were Depression days. Her father found it difficult to get employment in his profession in Western Australia, and, by 1940, was working as a barman for the Casa Degli Italiani Club in Fremantle. One day, without warning, the authorities came to his home.

> *I remember it was early in the morning and we were still in bed, my sisters and I, and these detectives came to our place. They turned everything upside down, the beds, all the mattresses upside down, the gloryboxes, they looked through all the linen, everywhere! And then they took my father away, because he was well known in Fremantle. Because he was so well known and so popular, they thought he might have something to do with giving information to the enemy.*

The detectives had their orders. They were to look for a radio, tuned in to enemy broadcasts, and presumably capable of transmitting secret information to the enemy at large. One of these policemen, although an Anglo-Australian, often went, socially, to the Club Giovane, one of Fremantle's two Italian Clubs. This club, unlike the Casa, was open to Australians and allowed the speaking of English. It became noticeably less Italian as the war went on.

Frances Iannello remembers that, following their father's internment, there was no money in the house. Neighbours helped but food was in short supply. Fish, usually plentiful in peacetime, was

Italian Fishing Boats, Fremantle.

denied them. Italian fishing boats were confiscated, often commandeered for war use or moored beyond their reach in the Canning River. Italian fishermen were forbidden to go near the shoreline to fish for their own families. The authorities believed that any venture out to sea raised the possibility of contact with foreign vessels and posed a risk to Australia's defence.

However, Frances and her family were able to make regular visits to their father in Fremantle prison. It was always a relief to find him alive and apparently well treated. Frances and her sisters cried every night at first, convinced that he would be shot for being 'a fascist'! Incidentally, they didn't know what that term meant. Fortunately her father proved no kind of political threat. Within three months he was free again. A different fate awaited her future brother-in-law, Frank Iannello, who was then working on the Fremantle wharves. He would spend most of the war behind barbed wire.

Joe Iannello is still angry about what happened to his older brother.

> I could not believe it. I couldn't understand why he or other people were interned, for the simple reason they were all family men, had sons and daughters and all that kind of thing. I could never remember them even talking about Italy, let alone doing anything! I think Australia made some horrible blues on that side.

The Iannello case was typical in its long-term effects; deeply scarring for many Italian families and disruptive of vital years of their lives. The authorities also commandeered their fishing boat, the *Dante*, without compensation, and the Iannello family income never fully recovered.

Joe Iannello, unlike his brother Frank, had been born in Australia in 1916. When he left school he handled a variety of jobs, but by the time war broke out he had been working as a barber for three years. By 1940 he was in full-time service with the

CMF, helping to defend Australia against its enemies. However, there was one unforeseen compensation for his enforced patriotism. Three years later, his stint in uniform over, he was back to his trade as a barber in Fremantle. One morning an army officer called into the shop, a colonel in the Intelligence section. Joe knew him well from his CMF days.

'Can you catch fish?' the officer asked gruffly.

'Well of course,' said Joe, 'but, as you know, we're not allowed to!'

That's all right! Here's a permit! My wife's ill, needs a special diet.'

On his first trip out, Joe caught far more than he, his family or the colonel's wife could eat. His friends had instructions to come round with buckets. Joe was able to keep families in fish for a long time after that, thanks to a bending of the rules. In fact the authorities had gradually realised that keeping Italian fishermen out of the water was having a negative effect on food production. Joe's bonus was part of that process.

Half a century later it is much easier to be critical of strict security regulations. With hindsight, internment looks like a heavy-handed government decree imposed by war upon the innocent and the suspect alike. The picture is all the more complex when seen from an Italian perspective. For many families there were divided loyalties and a genuine confusion of views.

Joe was one of three Iannello sons. Two were born in Australia, and the oldest, Frank, in Sicily. Their father, Cologero Iannello, had first come to Australia by accident. In Capo d'Orlando, his family had run a small fleet of sardine fishing boats. In 1896, with his brother, he set off from that port in a passenger vessel, intending to sail to the United States, still the preferred destination for most Italian emigrants.

For some reason, which his son Joe has never been able to discover, they found themselves in the waters of the southern hemisphere. Their boat broke down in mid-ocean and was towed to Sydney, a journey that took six months.

There Cologero abandoned the vessel and crossed the continent by land to join the small but increasing number of Italians who were beginning to fish the west coast of Australia for a living. Later he went back to Italy, served a four-year spell in the Italian navy, married and, in 1910, returned to Fremantle. His wife and eighteen-month-old son, Frank, joined him four years later. Two younger sons, Joe and Con, were born later in Australia.

By 1926 Cologero had become a naturalised Australian. Fourteen years later, when World War Two came to Australia, both younger sons, Joe and Con, were swiftly signed up for home-front defence, whereas the eldest, Sicilian-born Frank, was interned. Joe believes that the authorities acted against him, in part, because he was not a naturalised Australian citizen. He also believes Frank's own outspokenness at work could have drawn attention to himself. When overseas supplies, rope from Britain, cork from Spain and so on, failed to arrive at the wharf, Frank was wont to express the view that, 'If you had someone here like Mussolini here the goods'd be here by now.'

Understandably, Italo-Australians took a considerable interest in the Italy of the 1930s. When Frank Iannello spoke about Mussolini's achievements to others, his conversations were reported to the authorities. He hadn't realised that it was both dangerous and difficult to admire Il Duce's achievements so openly.

> At that time, to tell you the truth, I felt proud that Italy was making progress, regardless of what they said about Mussolini. The young people coming out before his time, they'd have a bit of a coat made by the village sarta, made of this brown cottony stuff and they looked very yokel-like. Whereas afterwards they were neatly dressed and I noticed this difference and it struck me.
>
> I was also very much impressed when Mussolini drained the Pontine marshes, and then reading that wheat production was far in excess of what we were pro-

ducing in Australia. Those things really impressed me. That was my only involvement.

Involvement that would prove costly.

Well, when I was interned, I think it was someone that dobbed me in that particular day, because months before we were talking about fascism in Italy and so forth. And I made this statement in front of this chap. He was a wharfie I think. And he said, 'What! You'd like us to have fascism here?' And I said, 'No! Not in the bloody race! I'm not suggesting that! But according to circumstances in Italy, I think it's done some good, y'know!'

So, the day before I was interned, I was on the jetty. I'd taken to fishing again. I saw him walk up the jetty. He looked at me. Well, he glared at me, you know! And the following day I was picked up.

Frank had no naturalisation papers. He had lived in Australia from infancy, had always assumed himself to be an Australian and registered accordingly on his father's papers. He occupied a responsible position as Head Traveller in the Union Stores on the Fremantle wharf, and in peacetime he would almost certainly have been given time to correct the anomaly. However, in 1940 the authorities enforced the strict letter of the law and Frank Iannello spent the rest of the war and more, as an internee. He used the time to write continuously to the authorities, protesting his innocence, but to no effect.

For a few, though, enthusiasm for Italian progress under Il Duce went well beyond interest and admiration, and where this happened, these individuals drew attention not only to themselves but also to the Italian community in general.

One woman, who prefers not to be named, is still bitter about her father's ardent fascism and its effect on her own childhood.

> *My father's political views changed when Mussolini and Hitler were building up the country. Fascism was brought inside our home. Every night before we went to bed we all had to line up and salute Il Duce! What effect did it have on me? It had a dreadful effect because we were only children. We were living in Australia and Australia was our country. And we wanted more than anything else to be like the rest of the children at school – the Australian children.*

For young Italo-Australians, the tension between belonging to a new generation and family pride in nationality was not easy to live with. As a teenager Nancy Fiocco, born and brought up in Fremantle, felt caught in the middle.

> *It was quite confusing because before that we were thinking about Mussolini and how brave he was and all this, and all of a sudden war breaks out and your loyalties had to change. Everybody was joining up. My brother felt quite confused and he thought his duty was to join up. I don't know how he felt about it personally, but I was quite confused about it and I thought: Here we are, We're Italians one moment and we're quite proud of Mussolini and next minute here's my brother going off to fight him!*

If it was confusing for the young, there were also pressures upon parents who chose to listen to the stirring messages from their homeland. Mussolini's government was making strenuous efforts to influence Italians abroad. From the late 1930s onwards, a succession of consuls in Perth were active promoters of the political benefits of Mussolini's new order. Some Italian consuls in other States, however, lacked zeal in their promotion of fascist ideals.

Within the Western Australian Italian community opinion

Mourners raise their arms in fascist salute during the funeral service of a fellow prisoner. Barmera, South Australia.

was divided. The Italian Club in Perth became a political arena where competing ideologies sought to dominate what was ostensibly a social club. Eventually an extreme right-wing group led by a P Sertorio broke away to found the Casa Degli Italiani in Fremantle.

This club celebrated Mussolini's triumphs in Abyssinia and earned the bitter hostility of Italians on the left of the political spectrum.

Australian authorities closed the Casa at the outbreak of war and arrested its leading officials. They were the first casualties of the internment policy.

Amidst the turmoil and confusion, a third, neutral, group became caught up in the ferment of declared war. These were Italians who had no interest in the politics of either right or left. They had come to Australia to work, save and, maybe, if successful, return to Italy.

Many of these settlers had come from rural regions where land was increasingly scarce and less viable as too many siblings competed for family inheritance. Emigration offered the prized opportunity to acquire and own land through hard work and perseverance. Beside this goal, the competing ideologies of the 1930s held little attraction.

As the international scene became more tense, it became obvious to Italian rural workers that it might be dangerous to return to Italy. They did not care about, or share, Mussolini's dreams of empire. Return for most was also a dream, given their income. More realistically they needed to know where they stood if war came. Many became naturalised Australians, both to protect themselves and because, as Australians, they could buy land from which to make a living.

However, becoming naturalised wasn't just a matter of filling in a form. For those working a market garden, like Adele Levis' family, money was the first problem.

To become naturalised it cost five pounds! Well, we didn't own the place we were living in! We were trying to make

27

a living on this leased land which cost a pound a week!
Now when you've got four small children, housed in a
corrugated shack, five pounds was five weeks rent. I can
remember my father was very, very concerned about what
could happen to us. We'd seen others interned and he
was a bit afraid that this situation could happen to us. It
would mean splitting up the family.

Now to work this land, to earn a living as a market
gardener those days, without tractors, you needed all the
helping hands you could get! It really would have been a
problem for our family if anyone of us was removed.

Adele's father, Angelo Levis, had been in Australia for fifteen
years. He had emigrated from the small village of Ponte Nelle Alpi
in the province of Billuno, north-east Italy. By 1939 the family ran
a market garden in the railway suburb of Bayswater, east of Perth.
Adele herself had left school at fourteen to help work the family
land. There were not enough hours in the day to do all the work
required, let alone time to take an interest in politics. Even if there
had been, Angelo himself had been sufficiently disillusioned by his
personal experience of World War One to hold any brief for politi-
cians like Mussolini.

Fortunately in his case, the authorities were humane and prag-
matic. Where Italians like the Levis family were obviously
hardworking and politically silent, they often left them alone.
Adele recalls the day they paid a visit.

I was out in the garden and two men came out from the
Immigration Department and asked if we were natu-
ralised. My father said 'No'. He was told that it might be
a good idea if he did. So my father subsequently did.

The Levis family escaped internment but were still strongly
aware of the threat to their freedom. At the age of sixteen, Adele
herself was fingerprinted and measured, a process which she still

recalls as embarrassing. The detective who took her prints was originally from Italy himself. He handled the process tactfully but Adele was, and is, still puzzled by the fact that he was part of the process of taking precautions against 'enemy aliens'. Along with other Italians they were not allowed to own a wireless lest they should listen to Axis propaganda.

In addition, each member of the family was issued with an identity card, complete with photograph, and instructed that they must report to the nearest police station if they travelled more than fifteen kilometres from their home. The latter precaution was irrelevant to a family which was trying to keep above the breadline, working all hours and seven days a week to grow and sell their produce.

Their efforts were an obvious contribution to wartime food production. Adele considers that helped them escape the fate of many others. In addition, their neighbours were supportive of their efforts and appreciative of their hard work. So while for much of the war the threat of internment hung over their heads, they had already earned the respect of people who knew them as a family.

Dominic Della Vedova had come to Australia from the small northern Italian village of Baruffini, not far from the city of Tirano, north-east of Milan. He had already seen action in one war. At seventeen he had gone to fight for Italy, then on the side of Britain and France against Germany. Dominic served for three years on the northern Italian front and then returned to Baruffini.

There he had worked as a small farmer, making a poor living from pieces of land, scattered here and there on the steep mountainsides. There simply wasn't enough land from which to make a good living.

There was a lot of talk in the village about Australia and the exciting prospects of finding gold. There, it seemed, you could save enough to return, buy land in Italy and, at last, prosper. Other members of Dominic's family had done just that and his own brother, Peter, had already left for Western Australia in 1923.

Abbondanza Vadala's Certificate of Registration of Alien.

30

However, it took a long time for Dominic to realise his ambition. When he arrived in Fremantle, in 1925, he took work anywhere he could find it, labouring in the Wheatbelt and down the goldmines in Kalgoorlie. He scraped and saved right through the Depression years. Meanwhile his wife, Elisabetta, son, Bill, and daughters, Maria and Josephine, remained in Baruffini trying to make a living as best they could. Italy was also in the grip of the Depression. As soon as he had reached his target Dominic intended to return to them.

That took six years. By 1931 he had the funds to go home and start a new life. But before he left Dominic went to say farewell to friends in the green, lush South-West. He saw country he'd never dreamed existed. This was the place to farm, not Baruffini. Dominic put his funds into a farm near Pemberton in the karri loam country, and wrote home. His family should come and join him in Australia. He took out Australian citizenship and awaited their arrival.

His son, Bill, came first and joined him on the farm in 1935. Two years later Elisabetta and the rest of the family stepped off the ship at Fremantle, on 17 August 1937. His daughter Josephine then greeted her father for the first time. She had been two when he left Italy and could scarcely remember him.

Australia seemed very strange to Josephine and Maria. They expected the shops in Fremantle to be glamorous and exciting, but, like much else in post-Depression Australia, their drab displays reflected the bleak time everyone had just come through. The bush, too, on the long railway journey down to Pemberton, seemed endless, broken only briefly by tiny settlements, pinpoints in an immense wilderness. However, there were ample compensations, a journey together through a new landscape, reunion with their beloved older brother, Bill, and delight in the new birdsongs and wildflowers of the karri country. The twelve years of separation fell away. The farm soon prospered and everybody adapted well to their new lifestyle.

We went to the farm and we were really happy there. We had Dad, we had Bill and we were a real family. We never even thought about going back to Italy. And we even forgot our friends and relations. At least we children did. For my mother it was different. But we were really happy.

However, their father worried about the turn of events in far-off Europe.

He would read the paper every night and he would talk about the things that Mussolini was doing with Hitler.

'He can't fight along with Germany! They won't do it! The Italians won't do it! I'm sure it's all a mistake.'

He still believed at the last minute, Italy would fight for the Allies. We never had a wireless. We didn't know the latest news but our neighbour called out to us from the other side of the fence, 'Italy's at war against the Allies!' Of course I remember Dad was very upset about this, but we had breakfast and went to work. We didn't pay much more notice.

And at lunchtime we heard a car, which was very unusual in them days to see a car coming up to the farm because it was always a horse and cart. And we all looked out and said, 'Oh look! That is the police there!' And Dad said, 'Well, let him come in, make him welcome.'

So as he comes in, he says, 'Are you Dominic Della Vedova?'

'Yes I am.'

'I have orders to arrest you!'

And, my dad, I could see him, he sort of changed colour, you know, and he said, 'Whatever for?' And the policeman said, 'It's not my fault. I don't really want to do this, but I have orders. Blame Hitler and Mussolini that they declared the war!' And Dad said, 'What have they got to do with me? I'm an Australian citizen!'

My mother came up then and said 'What's happen-
ing, Dad?' And Dad said, 'I have to go with the police!'
And we had to support Mum then because she just about
fainted because she said, 'Not after such a short time!'

Dominic Della Vedova left quietly. His son, Bill, went down to
the Pemberton railway station to see his father go and give him
some money for the journey. The policeman who'd arrested
Dominic in the first place, cut their goodbyes short, almost
slamming the carriage window down on Bill's outstretched hand
as the train began to move. He was escorting Dominic to prison
in Fremantle.

Dominic Della Vedova would not return to his South-West farm
until almost the end of the war. Elisabetta and his children had to
run the property as best they could without him.

Bill Della Vedova carried on his father's work of growing
potatoes and rearing cattle. He believed the authorities were convinced that his father was a fascist. In his view they found
difficulty in distinguishing between a point of view — his father
may have expressed admiration for something Mussolini had done
— and actual membership or advocacy of right-wing policies.

He also suspected that a chance remark, together with a grudge
held by one local policeman, may have brought suspicion upon his
father. Given Dominic Della Vedova's interest in Italian affairs, it
is easy to see how this could have happened.

To this day, his daughter, Josephine Cabassi, still does not know
why he was interned.

After he'd bought the farm he didn't give tuppence for
Mussolini. Italians all had a soft spot for Mussolini
before the war, but once he was here Dad was far too
busy just making a living from the land and being with
his family again.

33

The authorities never gave reasons for Dominic Della Vedova's internment, and Josephine reflects now that the family was under too much pressure just surviving, in his absence, to write and seek explanations.

> *I think we failed there. We should have gone and made ourselves known to the authorities. But we were on a farm and we lacked quite a bit of education. We didn't know how to go about it. And of course if we had spoken English fluently, we would have been listened to. But if you don't, they just listen and they say, 'Forget about it!'*

Many sympathetic friends and neighbours, shocked by Dominic Della Vedova's sudden removal, signed a petition for his release. It had no effect.

After three months imprisonment in Fremantle, Dominic Della Vedova, along with many more internees, was sent to Harvey Internment Camp, a hundred and twenty kilometres south of Perth. It was still a long way, however, for the Della Vedova family to come up from Pemberton in the far South-West. But at least they could now see their father.

> *And when you went to the gate to go inside there was a high building there with two or three machine-guns, pointing out of the windows. It was frightening for us the first time we went to see him. The machine-guns give you a terrible feeling. But the soldiers, they were exceptionally good. If you went to see Dad you had to get a permit, and you presented it and they were so kind and very polite.*
>
> *And when we saw Dad, we had an emotion in our throat, we couldn't speak. We tried to touch him. First thing he asked was how was the farm going, how were all the animals that he loved so much. Of course we were able to tell him that we were managing all right.*

Mick Cabassi (who later married Josephine Della Vedova) planting
potatoes on the family farm.

The town of Harvey shelters in a broad valley, running west from the Darling Ranges. The site chosen for the internment camp lay in a pleasant fold in the hills just north of the town. In 1940 Madge Johnston lived opposite the newly constructed prison.

> *Like all camps, barbed wire everywhere. Four huge towers with searchlights that went all night. That used to bug me because we were so close to it. We could always hear the noise from the camp. It was a sad cheerless place I think.*

In the early years of the war Harvey came to play gaol to part of its own population. Like Waroona, Yarloop and several other small towns along the edge of the Darling Ranges, Harvey had then, and still has, a sizeable but largely apolitical Italian population. In the early 1940s it would have been very hard to find an agitator amongst them. They were too busy growing fruit and vegetables or working for others on rural properties. Although many had arrived only recently, Italians were an accepted part of the local scene. They kept themselves to themselves but there was no friction in the community.

Max Baker was fourteen in 1940 and lived in the small dairy town of Waroona, just north of Harvey. He was to witness the first internment action.

> *Quite suddenly the militia comes marching into town. As a young boy I thought they were fairly old-looking blokes with rifles and stuff like that. And they then assembled near the recreation ground and we were all quite intrigued as to what was going on, and we were suddenly told they were going to round up all the Italians, and over the next week that's what happened. There was no violence, none whatever. A lot of crying but not because of anything that the militia did, It was a very emotional thing, because they had to leave their properties.*
>
> *They were just taken off. They had potato crops in,*

36

'To dear father, sending you kisses from afar. Lucy Rotondella.'

they had dairy cattle, they had pumpkin crops in. *There was irrigation water there to turn on and turn off and they could really see their life's work and lifestyle going down the drain.*

Max Baker also went to the Waroona cinema during the first week of the round-up.

Picture night in Waroona was Thursday night and of course everybody went to it. And of course the round-up was the talking point of the town, how everything was going, internment etc. I got to the pictures that night with my usual gang. We sat down. After a while this lone little Italian walked in. We knew him as Joe. And he sat down and looked furtively around for a while. And then I saw the local policeman, Fred Hearn. He was there with his wife and their baby.

Suddenly Fred's eyes caught Joe and everybody watched the little scenario that took place. And Fred walked over to Joe and said, 'Eh Joe! You should be over the road,' indicating where the recreation ground was, where they were holding all the internees. And little Joe looked up at Fred and said, 'Oh Mr Hearn I don't mind being interned but, please couldn't you just wait and let me see Hopalong Cassidy for the last time?'

But Fred was unrelenting. He said, 'No, Joe, Over you go!' And he escorted him out of the hall and over the road in complete silence. There was no clapping, no cheering, just complete silence. I think that shows how we felt about it!

Maria Baggetta, then Maria Panetta, and aged fourteen, had come to Australia in 1937 from the attractive coastal village of Sidorno Marina in the province of Calabria. Her father had first come in 1925, and his family followed him twelve years later.

Initially they lived in poor housing in Harvey where Maria remembers her mother crying for the country she had left behind. Fortunately, by 1940, they had become naturalised Australians and escaped internment. Maria witnessed their neighbours' surprise and shock when the militia marched into Harvey and took the men away.

> *There was one big revolution all over town, poor wives crying, mothers! It was very difficult for them to accept. Some of them had come to Australia only a few months before and all of a sudden their husbands, their fathers and their brothers were taken away and they were very distressed.*

As one of the few in her community who could speak English, Maria found herself acting as an interpreter, trying to explain what had happened to bewildered and shocked families. There was no way she herself could make sense of what had happened.

In many ways the strain was greater for those outside the barbed wire and tall towers of the internment camp than for those inside. Wives now had to cope with managing a property or running a business, as well as bringing up their families, coping with government authorities and visiting their husbands whenever possible. Families themselves were sometimes divided by the process. The police sergeant at Harvey was obliged to ensure the internment of his own son-in-law, who came from an immigrant family.

For the internees one of the main problems was boredom. They had little else to complain of materially. The food, by wartime standards, was good and often supplemented by little extras from home. And while prison routine was monotonous it was not exhausting. One or two internees ensured that it was sometimes entertaining. Dominic Baggetta, then only seventeen, regularly turned roll calls into chaos.

That's when the fun came. They counted us. They put
us in threes and they started to count from one end.
When they counted 'One, two, three. One, two, three',
somebody would bend down and there were two, not three
there. As soon as they'd passed, they stood up. One day
they finished the count with three or four missing.
'Where are they?' they wanted to know. They started
counting again, they counted again and sometimes it was
dinnertime and we were still there!

Dominic and his father had originally come from Siderno
Superiore, not far from Maria Panetta's village in Çalabria. They
roughed it to begin with in Australia, sleeping in tents and hay-
barns and taking any work they could find in the country. By 1940
they had settled in Harvey and had the beginnings of a potato-
growing business. That was now on hold.

John Mazzo, whose family lived in Harvey during the war,
remembers how one young and totally-free Italian, Joe Vozzo, even
tried to have himself interned. He was a tailor who lived in the
little timber town of Yarloop, not far from the Harvey camp, where
all his friends had gone. Life became extremely lonely after their
departure.

He asked the authorities for permission to join them. They told
him firmly to go away. They had no wish to intern him.
Undaunted, and genuinely affronted by the incarceration of his
companions, Joe decided to conduct a one-man demonstration.

So this particular Saturday afternoon, he got onto his
motorbike. He had a BSA motorbike I can remember
that. And the camp was situated alongside a rather steep
hill on the main highway. So what he decided to do was
to go up on his motorbike and do the fascist salute as he
passed the camp. He thought, 'This will stir the authori-
ties up.' And, naturally, not only did it stir up the
Australian authorities but it also brought a loud cheer

Portrait of Dominic Della Vedova drawn by a German internee at Loveday Camp, South Australia.

*from the Italian internees. So he said, 'Right, I'll go
again next Saturday.' This time the internees knew something was up because they were ready for him, hundreds
of them, lining the fence, cheering him.*

The Australian guards remained impassive during his first
'freedom ride', but during his second freedom ride they noted his
bike's registration number. At his third encore a week later, the
militia took pity on him. They came out and clapped him behind
the wire. Inside the camp, Joe Vozzo maintained his rage at the
mass internment of his comrades continuously protesting to the
authorities about being given no reason for their loss of liberty.

The government had justified internment as being 'in the national
interest'. However, the imprisonment of Italians from the rich
fruit, vegetable and dairy districts of the Harvey and Waroona
areas soon reduced the rate of wartime food production.

With so many able-bodied men out of action, crops rotted or
could not be harvested and stock went untended. Fortunately, it
did not take long for the authorities to recognise their mistake,
quietly releasing many of the local internees.

Max Baker saw them slip back into Waroona.

*Suddenly they're back. There was no announcement, no
nothing. Suddenly Joe and Lou and Charlie and everybody were back in town. I think the authorities suddenly
discovered they were more help to them outside than they
were inside because they were very, very vital people in
the food supply.*

Dominic Baggetta was out after three months and went straight
back to work, growing potatoes with his father.

Several Italian market gardeners from Perth had been interned and
were also released at this time. Part of their work in the camp had
been to grow vegetables for various Australian army camps. There

*Lt. Palmer inspecting cases of tomatoes picked by prisoners of war,
Murchison Camp, Victoria.*

was a pay-off after their release. Some obtained contracts to continue to supply the Australian army with tomatoes and other vegetables.

Other internees, however, were not so lucky. They were to stay behind the wire almost until the end of the war. Detention in Harvey, although it took its toll, had become bearable. There at least the prisoners had received regular visits from family and friends. However, there were other plans for them.

In April 1942 it had become alarmingly obvious that the Japanese could mount an invasion or a coastal attack on the Western Australian coast. They had already bombed Darwin. Japanese fighters had strafed flying boats off Broome and there had been other raids even further south. The Japanese navy was active off the north-west coast, and their aircraft carriers were investigating landing sites on the south coast of Western Australia.

Since the Harvey camp was only twenty kilometres from the west coast, and its powerful searchlights could easily be seen from the sea, the military decided to move all the internees inland. They feared that fifth columnists inside or outside the camp at Harvey could aid an enemy landing. The prisoners were to go, first to inland Kalgoorlie and later to Loveday in Riverland, South Australia, not far from Lake Bonnie. They went in great secrecy and with no warning.

Madge Johnston woke up one morning and noticed how quiet it was.

> *No one was told. All the internees were moved out at half-past three or four in the morning. They were marched into town to a train. Nobody in town knew about that.*

The prisoners travelled under cover of darkness to Kalgoorlie, a long, slow journey over the Darling Ranges and across back country routes into the Wheatbelt. Frank Iannello was on that train as it wound its way eastwards along branch routes through the bush.

Around midday, some ten hours or so after leaving Harvey, the train pulled into Narrogin. It was a planned meal stop.

As it happened, one of Frank's brothers, Con Iannello, serving in the CMF, had just been posted on light duties to Narrogin. His task that day was to feed the prisoners on that train.

> *I didn't realise at first what the train was. When it eventually did come, it was the internees coming from Harvey and that was where I saw my brother. The train was absolutely crowded and one of the chaps with me, he was a Greek as a matter of fact, he was absolutely devastated when I saw my brother. And we hugged one another. And the sergeant at the back saw us and yelled out something. I couldn't hear what it was with all the confusion on the train. I think we were giving out buns and fruit. We were all giving out different things.*
>
> *Then I met a couple of chaps who tried to tell me, 'Give a message to my wife! Give a message to my mother!' And this is going on right through the train. In the carriage I was serving in there would have been at least twenty people that I knew. I think they were mostly very frightened!*

And with good reason. Even if they held no fears for their own safety, they had no idea where they were going. Their interim destination was Kalgoorlie, some five hundred kilometres inland. The internees were being moved out of reach of their families.

Joe Iannello, Frank Iannello's other brother, was also serving with the CMF. He heard where Frank was being held and went to the Goldfields.

> *We went up to see him and it was the worst winter that Kalgoorlie had ever had. We had no money and we had to walk to the camp. It rained and blew and we were wet from head to foot and full of red mud. Anyhow we got there and they eventually brought my brother out. They*

45

*had us on one side of the table. My brother was a fair
distance away on the other side and we had the guards
there listening to every word you said. There I met
Captain Robinson, one of my captains from the Third
Field Artillery and he asked me what I was doing there.
I said, 'I've come up to see my brother.' He said 'Who is
your brother?' I said, 'Frank Iannello.' He couldn't believe
it, he absolutely couldn't believe it. He was absolutely
taken aback and he said, 'Are you sure Frank's your
brother?' I said, 'Of course he's my brother!'*

The next stop for Frank Iannello, Dominic Della Vedova and
for many other internees from all over Australia, was Loveday
Camp in Riverland, South Australia. For most, Loveday was as far
as they could be from their own homes.

In his new prison, Frank Iannello occupied himself in fighting
his own case for release, and acting as an unofficial secretary for
other internees. Many could not speak or write English. Frank
wrote and forwarded letters for them to the International Red
Cross, arguing their case or improving their contact with their
own famiies.

As the war slowly turned against the Axis powers, the
Australian authorities began to relax their detention of internees.
Nonetheless, many men in Loveday had to wait until war's end
before they regained their liberty.

Homecoming was quiet for most. Frank Iannello travelled alone
by train, across the recently cleared spaces of the Western
Australian Wheatbelt, down through the jarrah and wandoo
forests of the Darling Range, and, as the train pulled parallel with
the coast at Cottesloe, he saw the Indian Ocean again for the first
time in five years.

*You know, I felt as if I was afraid of the sea, it looked
that enormous. And I'd been a fisherman! And it looked
that enormous to me. I thought, I've got to sail on that!*

46

Dominic Della Vedova was released from Loveday in June 1944. He had been in prison for over three years. He too made the long journey back to Perth by slow train. Three hundred and fifty kilometres south, on the farm at Pemberton, the family waited. Josephine recalls that Dominic's dog knew his master was coming home.

> He got off a truck at the farm gate and the old dog was crying all the time. He'd cried all the time from the gate up to the house. That was a happy moment anyway.

She also knew what internment had cost her father.

> That experience was always with him. He wasted forty-four months of his life. He must have suffered a tremendous disappointment, being interned, because he was really in the prime of his life.

Even after his return, Dominic Della Vedova was not allowed to resume work on his farm for a further six months. He was compelled to work in the Civil Alien Corps in the timber mill at Pemberton. The authorities still had their eye on him.

Internment continued to cause divisions well after the war within the Italian community itself. Those released early had a head start in rebuilding their lives, and some who came out later resented the better fortune of those released earlier.

The whole business had been bewildering, wasteful, frustrating and frightening. Could it have been worse? Was it justified?

Dominic Della Vedova's daughter, Josephine Cabassi, acknowledged that the family suffered.

> But then it was wartime! And everybody suffers during the war. Being interned is not as bad as losing a family in death or anything like that. It was very sad. People lose a brother or a sister, a father. It's war and it's sad. It's like that for lots of people. It was wartime.

Dominic and Elisabetta Della Vedova with Rosh, the dog which welcomed Dominic home from prison.

Dominic Baggetta, rural worker from Waroona was interned for only three months. He was philosophical.

> *After all we was enemy. And they had always the right to put us there but we didn't deserve that because we come to Australia to do our work, make a few bob. If we could go back to our own country we would. If not we try to bring our family to Australia. But I tell you another thing! Say if the Australians had been interned in Italy, they might have been worse off than I was.*

Many Australians were interned in Italy, as it happened, but, unlike Dominic Baggetta, not as civilians. They went as military prisoners, captured in North Africa and sent to Italy. Italian soldiers, also taken captive in North Africa, were sent to Australia as prisoners of war.

Giuseppi Pallotta, Ted Mouritz, Tony Mouritz, Elio Amorozi with the family pets of the Mouritz farm.

THEY WERE REALLY GOOD FRIENDS

Italian POWs in Australia

They took us out to work. We built fences, cut fence posts, all sorts of jobs, looking after the sheep, ploughing with the tractor. We learnt how to do all those sorts of jobs.

POW Giuseppe (Joe) Varone

Everything worked fine. The farmer was bound to the prisoner and the prisoner bound to the farmer. We all worked together. For my part I didn't find in Australia that I was a prisoner and the boss was a boss. I found a friend.

POW Luigi Bassano.

Italian soldiers Giuseppe Varone and Luigi Bassano became prisoners of war during the Libyan campaign in 1942 and both men were to spend the rest of their war in Australia. They were just two of thousands of Italian soldiers who spent much of their war on Australian farms.

Their story is quite distinct from the story of civilian internees. However, there were fleeting contacts. Some internees remember snatches of conversation with their ex-compatriots in uniform, hastily shouted exchanges as trains passed each other in the countryside. To many civilian onlookers or casual witnesses, there was little distinction between military and civilian prisoners. They were simply Italians in different uniforms. But, for their part, prisoners of war were unwilling immigrants who never expected to end up in Australia.

After capture and forced marches through North Africa they were shipped to India and held in camps in Bombay for twelve months. There was little to do there. The heat, the quality of their food and the unfamiliar conditions began to take their toll on morale. The men were idle and listless. At the same time Australia had sent many of its own men away to the war in Europe, the Middle East and elsewhere. Within rural Australia there was now an acute labour shortage. For these reasons the Allied authorities decided to move their Italian prisoners to a

An Italian being captured in North Africa by an Australian soldier.

better climate and conditions. So Australia became a host to over ten thousand Italian and German POWs.

Italian POWs in Western Australia were housed in a bush prison at Marranup, not far from the civilian internment camp at Harvey. However the authorities had learnt one important lesson from the internment experience; that it did not help the war effort to keep rural workers away from the land. The military acknowledged this point right from the arrival of their POWs. Farm work would not only assist the war effort, it would cut down on the cost of keeping soldiers as prisoners. The government had Italian and not German POWs in mind. German POWs, many of whom held strong Nazi views, were not regarded as suitable for rural work among Australian families. Italians were given the choice. They were not compelled to do rural work but most jumped at the chance to get away from the monotony of camp life.

The army set up labour centres in the larger country towns; distribution points to supervise the new rural work force. Each centre had a captain, a private and an interpreter.

Wheatbelt farmer Mick Mouritz, from the Hyden district in the southern Wheatbelt , was one of the first to take in POWs.

> *On a certain day you'd go into the centre and the captain would show you the prisoners and you'd take your pick. And you could always send them back if they didn't work out.*

Doreen and Arthur Marsh, who also farmed near Hyden had agreed to take a couple of POWs and were later to receive Giuseppe Varone. They took their little son, Neville, with them to meet their first batch of prisoners.

> *We went into Hyden at night-time, and our boy, was just a little fellow, and they were striking matches to see his face. You know they were all so thrilled to see his face.*

In taking on prisoners, some farming families, like the Marshes, were also taking on an extra workload. On their newly established farm, there was no water heater and no large supply of water. They had to heat every drop in a copper both for washing and cooking. Besides their own family they now had two extra men whose dusty clothes joined the family wash pile.

Pasquale Amato came from a small village, Grassano, in the southern region of Basilicata. His family was in the transport business, carrying goods to local ports with bullock and horse teams. Conscripted into the army, he was one of many Italian soldiers sent to North Africa. In early January 1941 he and his brother, Giuseppe, were captured by Australian troops at Bardia and taken to Egypt. Their second destination was India where the brothers were to separate. Giuseppe remained in India but Pasquale chose to go to Australia. He arrived in Melbourne on 4 June 1944. His first working assignment was in the orchard area of Shepparton, northern Victoria. There he worked for a short spell picking oranges and other fruit.

Almost at random, it seemed, he was then sent west, travelling across the Nullarbor by train, first to Perth and then to the Great Southern wheat and wool area, east of the Perth-Albany railway. Farms in Western Australia were urgently in need of labour.

> I arrived there in the night. I couldn't see anything. It was all bush, where I was sent, to Tambellup, sixty miles, bush after bush. In the morning when I woke up I could see cows and sheep.

Pasquale saw little of his employer. His first job was picking mallee roots. Soon he was working a long day, starting up the tractor at seven in the morning and ploughing until dark fell. He returned to sleep in a hut away from the farmhouse. The farmer cooked for them both, serving up good food but not

Pasquale Amato, Grassano, Italy, before the outbreak of World War Two.

table companionship. Pasquale ate his meals alone on the verandah. That was also where the farmer gave him infrequent and clumsy hair cuts. He was also unable to go to Mass, which for Pasquale was an important part of his week. His employer would not take him to church or to get his hair cut in the nearest town. These arrangements were not privileges, they were rights under the arrangement made with rural employers for POW labour.

Pasquale soon absconded, hiding out under a water tank for almost forty-eight hours. It was the only way he felt he could protest. The military authorities transferred him further east to the Great Southern town of Gnowangerup. There he was to work for the Garnett family.

> This Garnett he was a family man. He liked to see his work done. On the first day he said to me, 'You go much for politics?' I said, 'Yes, I go for my politics and I keep mine to myself.' And he said, 'If you want to be my friend, put politics out. I keep my politics. You keep yours.'

The Garnetts were strict Baptists, and Pasquale Amato, Catholic and politically to the right. However, throughout the war and long after, they put politics and religion aside in favour of respect and tolerance. Nevertheless the tension that war brought would remain with many Australian families and their guests for much of that time. On the one hand the POWs were naturally anxious for news of the war, while their hosts didn't care much for talk of the achievements of Mussolini. The war stood like a barrier between them.

Pasquale Amato felt that Australia was:

> Full of propaganda. If Mr Churchill had told them that donkeys flew, Australians would have believed him.

Top: Pasquale Amato in India after his capture.
Bottom: Pasquale Amato with Glenys Garnett.

Nevertheless, Glen and Gladys Garnett made him welcome on their farm. They made a room for him in an old house adjacent to the main homestead and sheds, but he ate with the family and soon befriended both their baby daughter, Glenys, and Horace, the family kangaroo dog. Horace slept at the end of Pasquale's bed, and, when cold, alongside his new mate.

Irene Falconer and her husband were to take POWs onto their farm very late in the war. They needed rural help for their isolated farm near Bridgetown. John Falconer had already been manpowered to the Bridgetown powerhouse as part of the war effort, and the Falconers had only been able to obtain the farm on condition that John took charge of the local dehydrator and prepared dried and tinned apples for the army. In his absence, Irene had to work the farm on her own for much of the time. So the Falconers applied for POWs to help her out.

> And on the 27 of March 1945, which was a shockingly hot day and we were fighting a bushfire on two sides of our property – there was forest on each side – the control centre rang to say our first prisoner had arrived and would we come and get him.
>
> 'Leave the bushfire, it will be all right. Come and get your prisoner,' which, of course, we couldn't do.
>
> But later in the day we received Carlos Formonte. Carlos was a nineteen-year-old. He had been captured in Libya and held a prisoner of war there, and then brought out to the concentration camp which was at Harvey, and he was there for some time.

Carlos, a small man, was a trainee chef, or had been until the war cut short his culinary hopes. To the delight of the Falconers' son, John, Carlos made him a semi-permanent loan of an extra pair of size five boots, hobnailed and horseshoe-heeled footwear, in which John could strut the corridors of Bridgetown State school. Boots, especially those of army quality, were a mark of status for any schoolkid in wartime Australia.

The potential chef kept his hand in on the farm. During the week he fed young John Falconer on Australian country fare, thick slices of bread with home-cured bacon, tomato and cheese, toasted in the Metters oven. Sunday, however, was a day for Italian dishes. Carlos was allowed to invite prisoners from surrounding farms to join the family in the backyard. These were mighty feasts, as young John Falconer recalls them. At these gatherings he was supposed to help the prisoners improve their command of English but the most enduring Sunday school lesson was his own acquisition of the noble, if slippery art of cooking spaghetti.

John still remembers the recipes.

> The best ingredients, including farm-fresh eggs, were used. The paste was rolled into flat sheets, cut into strips, and hung to dry. When cooked it was eaten with a fork, of course. The authentic, delicious sauce, seemed to bubble away all day. Tomatoes, herbs, garlic, all cooked down to a mouth-watering sauce, while the men stood around the backyard copper talking.

His mother, Irene, who regularly bought the spaghetti and cheese herself, saw her effort rewarded.

> They used a lot, and lardo (that was lard) they used that for all their cooking because it had a nicer flavour than butter. They never tasted anything on the way. They would smell it, and they'd keep on smelling this sauce and when it had the right smell then it was ready. The spaghetti was cooked for only twenty minutes at the end of which time it was ready for eating. They used to have their plates piled up, and the way they ate it, they said, was because they ate it quickly. They didn't chew it up, it just slid down.

Top: Carlos Formonte, who worked on Irene and John Falconer's farm, dressed as a tea lady.
Bottom: John Falconer (left) with Carlos Formonte and Giuseppe (Joseph) Chianisi who are wearing clothes bought by Irene Falconer.

On an average weekend ten POWs, together with their new apprentice chef, John Falconer, got through an entire twenty-two pound pinewood box of spaghetti. And somehow, that other indispensable accompaniment of Italian cuisine, wine, made an unconventional appearance. There were as many varieties as there were fruits in season. Juices were squeezed through clean flourbags and the liquid simply bottled.

John himself took pear wine to school, an action which shortened his academic career but gave him more time to catch 'underground mutton' which went well with the spaghetti on Sundays.

Later the Falconers applied for another prisoner. They acquired Giuseppe Chianisi.

> Carlos and Giuseppe – Joseph (as we called him). Joseph was a very big man and Carlos was very small. Carlos mainly worked with the stock and Joseph worked in the orchard. Joseph had been in the Department of Agriculture in Italy. He and my husband were picking apples one day and he said to John, 'I pick this one,' and John said, 'Yes, that's a Granny,' and he said, 'No, Mr John, not a Granny.' He said, 'Well, it's supposed to be a Granny.' He said, 'No, is no Granny.'
>
> When John looked at it he discovered there was a difference but it was very difficult to tell, and I don't know where he went for advice, but he found out that Joseph was right. So he knew his agriculture, or at least he knew his apples.

He also knew animal husbandry, as it turned out. He could deliver calves and manage livestock very competently. This was just as well, given John Falconer's frequent absence at the Bridgetown powerhouse. The army had warned the Falconers that POWs would not work for a woman but Irene had no trouble.

People said I was crazy because our farm was called 'The Hollow' and it was in a hollow. There were other farms around, but we were a bit out of sight. But I had no trouble whatever with either of those men. We treated them as human beings, as equals, because I used to say to them I thought women were good diplomats for peace. I said that if things were reversed and my son was a prisoner of war in their country, if they would remember the treatment they got at our place, you know, it might make all the difference. I had no bother whatsoever with either of the men.

Doreen Marsh remembers another farmer, in the Hyden district, who insisted on treating the POWs like enemies, keeping them very much at a distance, both physically and mentally.

They reckoned they were fighting against our men, that sort of thing.

For their part, the Marsh family wanted to form relationships with Giuseppe Varone and the other prisoners who came to their farm.

As far as we were concerned they were human beings and we treated them as we would any other employee.

The Varones farmed land in the Monte Cassino region, west of the Appennines and on the road north to Rome. Giuseppe Varone had not seen his wife, Filomena, and his children since the outbreak of war.

During the war, however, he was to find a substitute family with the Marshes of Hyden. He spoke almost no English when he came but help was already at hand. Doreen Marsh was a correspondence course teacher and had previously helped a Russian

*Giuseppe Varone on the back of the truck while working on the
Marsh farm.*

neighbour on a nearby farm to learn English. She was quite ready to take on new pupils.

> They would learn a few words of English and likewise we'd learn a few words of Italian and we'd be able to fill in. They used to get the Italian papers and I would read quite a lot. And of course there were words that were similar, like cavolfiore for cauliflower and simpatico for sympathy. We also used to speak pidgin to them, cut out unnecessary words.

Later, when the war had ended, Doreen would help Giuseppe Varone's son, Gerado, learn English when he came to Australia.

Farmer's wife, Gwen Slarke, from Lake Grace, south-east of Hyden, and her husband also talked a kind of pidgin language to their two POWs. It had an interesting side effect on their own discourse.

> We found we were speaking to one another of an evening, as we had been talking to the prisoners all day – to try and make the conversation easy.

However, the Slarkes were to be outdone by one local, the Lake Grace doctor. She took full advantage of an Italian presence in the district.

> She could speak Italian and she was most interested in the prisoners of war. And when they went to her she had every sympathy for them. And much to the nurses' disgust she used to put them into hospital where they were short staffed and they resented this rather. But the doctor's word was law and in the hospital the prisoners would have to stay. And she wanted them there so that she could try her Italian out on them.

However, language led Irene Falconer, in her own words,

... into trouble because I never swore but I used to say, 'Swine!' and if you can put as much into an ordinary word, you might as well swear, I suppose. I'd get exasperated sometimes with Carlos and I'd say, 'Ooh you little swine!' He thought it was a term of praise and then he went into what they called the canteen after Mass. They collected down there, had a talk for a little while to their mates and then came back home, or were supposed to come back home. He went one Sunday and they were all talking about their various bosses and some of them treated them similar to dogs. They used to mutter about being called dogs. And he said his Madame was very genteel, very genteel.

He said, 'She call me little swine,' and the only fascist amongst them was on the farm next to us, and he was a horrible creature, and he said, 'Little swine!' he said, 'Those are pigs!' That offended Carlos greatly so he came home and if he was in a bit of a paddy he would knock on the door, and I could always tell by that knock that there was something wrong. So I went to the door and said, 'What is wrong?' and he said, 'You call canteen, Madame. I go back in camp.' I said, 'Oh, when are you going?' He said, 'You call canteen,' and I said, 'Oh, all right. Why?'

Then he explained that he thought I meant something nice and it was horrible. He wasn't standing that, he was going back in camp. So I said, 'All right.'

So away he went. He would pack his things. They had a room, a very nice room, the best on the farm and it was away from the house but it was a complete room. It had a fireplace and a mantelpiece, chairs and a table and so on, a bed. Anyhow sometime later he came back and it was a different knock on the door, and he had a

> bunch of flowers. If ever he wanted to make his peace
> with me he went round the garden and picked some
> flowers. So he was standing at the door and he said, 'You
> call canteen?' and I said, 'No.' He said, 'All right, I not
> go.' He said, 'This for you.' So that was all right.

However, personal relationships didn't always develop between host and prisoner. On their four-thousand-acre farm at Meckering, a few kilometres east of York, Prudence and Roy Broad employed POWs and were later to take in Luigi Bassano. They were well aware that, in their district, some Italians were not so warmly welcomed.

> One farmer used to treat his POWs badly. He reckoned
> they'd been fighting against our men or something like
> that. They didn't live in on the farm. He used to take
> them out rations. We had two that had been working for
> this same man and they told us that some days there was
> no bread, some days no tea, some days no sugar.

Gwen Slarke and her husband rapidly abandoned their original intentions for their POWs.

> When they first came we thought they'd be best on their
> own and we served their meals out on the verandah, but
> they wouldn't eat it. And I said to my husband one day,
> 'We'll have to bring the boys inside and have their meals
> with us.' They came to our table and they'd eat every-
> thing that was put in front of them.

For Luigi Bassano the friendship the Broad family showed him went a long way to make up for the family he had left behind in the small Adriatic fishing village of San Vito, in the province of Chieti in the Abruzzi region. Luigi came from a family of fisher-men and plied that trade as well as any other work that came his way. He had been born in Buenos Aires because his father, as a

Prudence, Pam and Des Broad with the prisoners of war who worked on their farm, Luigi Bassano and Paolo Rubinich.

young married man, had gone off alone to Argentina to improve his fortune. His wife, fearing she might lose him, then took ship to South America herself. Eventually the family returned to San Vito.

In 1930 Luigi married his former sweetheart, Maria Irlandini. They had known each other ever since primary school days and married at nineteen. The couple had two daughters, Anna and Vita, born in 1931 and 1934. By 1937 it was harder to get regular jobs of any kind. Luigi had to leave his family and take work in Libya where Mussolini's imperial ventures had the side effect of providing work for some of his countrymen. Luigi took work as a canteen cook, providing meals for the Italian army. Within a year he had been conscripted into the army itself.

In 1941 Luigi Bassano became a prisoner of war during the North African campaign. The British sent him first to Egypt and later to India. Maria had no news of him for three months, apart from one Red Cross letter posted in Egypt. There were no letters from India and it was not until Luigi eventually arrived in Fremantle that Maria knew what had become of him. His letters from Meckering, censored by the authorities, could tell her little of the friendship that he had now found with the Broads.

> I am well. I hope you and the children are well.
> I will write to you again.

Bruno Anghinetti, from the village of Riano near Parma, had left his relations behind in northern Italy. He also had the good fortune to find a friendly Australian family. Conscripted into the Italian army in 1937, he was to see his family and the woman he later married, Rena Gonizzi, only once in the next seven years. Briefly discharged in 1938, he was reconscripted in 1940 and captured in Libya in 1941.

Bruno spent the first months of his imprisonment in Egypt. Later his contingent went on to India where the climate brought ill health and death to many of his fellow captives. Seventy-five men died from disease in Bruno's camp alone.

Later the POWs were sent to various countries. Bruno could have ended up in South Africa or England, but, for reasons that weren't clear at the time, he landed in Fremantle on 12 January 1944 after two and a half years of captivity.

His batch of POWs went to Busselton, in the south-west of Western Australia. If he thought at all about Australians, Bruno had expected them to be black people. (Much of Mussolini's propaganda about Australian soldiers stressed that they were child eaters and rapists.)

However, he found himself allocated to the Smith family at nearby Jindong. Stephen Smith, then nineteen, had been manpowered during the war to remain and help with farm work. His father had been gassed in World War One and couldn't run the property on his own. They were still short-handed and were pleased to hear that they might now acquire two POWs.

For his part, Bruno feared that he might be placed with another POW from Southern Italy with whom he did not get on. Stephen remembers Bruno's plea, through the interpreter, that if they would take him by himself, he would do the work of two men.

First thing at Jindong the Smiths offered him a cup of tea and then, an hour or so later, invited him to join the family for their evening 'tea'. It was Bruno's first brush with the intricacies of Australian culture. However, within three or four weeks he would make himself understood and understand instructions. Later, on that first evening, Stephen unrolled the world map and they looked up Bruno Anghinetti's birthplace, almost half a world away.

There was plenty of work for the man who had promised to do the work of two. The Smiths had only just begun to develop their farm. There were potatoes to plant and cows to milk, work that Bruno had done before. However, splitting posts was a new task. His new work partner and, soon, friend, Stephen Smith showed him how.

Stephen learned Italian and Bruno, English, exchanging vocabulary, the words for axe and mattock, hammer and nails, open and shut, gate and fence; essential terms for the jobs to be done but also an enjoyable part of the work itself.

Stephen can still speak Italian, if a little rustily, and Bruno, who arrived in Australia with only 'Yes' and 'No' learned his English out in the paddock. Much later he had the Smiths in stitches when they were moving furniture together in the farmhouse. 'Take care with that dressing-table, Bruno. If you break the mirror it means seven years bad luck!'

Bruno expressed mock horror. 'You mean seven years in Australia?'

For pioneer Wheatbelt farmers like Mick Mouritz, relationships grew through the work he found for his prisoners.

> My chief interest in employing them was that the year before I had ploughed up about two hundred acres of country that was loaded with stones and roots, very rough country. And I had an idea that if I got the prisoners I could clean it up. Well, they spent three months carting the stones and roots off that paddock and I gradually got to know them. One was a builder and the other a farmhand.
>
> When I'd done most of the rough work round the farm I found myself in a position to build a house. The POWs had already made six thousand cement bricks for me. They seemed to be in their element doing that. And when the bricks were finished, the builder sent word he couldn't be along for about six months. One of the prisoners suggested to me 'Why boss you not let me build you this house. We understand this.' And the upshot was that they built a beautiful home for me. And it stands today as a monument to Italian POWs in Australia.

Italian prisoners, for the most part, were willing to work hard.

Their energy earned a measure of reward. For men, far from their own families and friends, building homes, even if they were for other people, exchanging language and making friends with the farmers' children were all part of that process.

Many farmers' wives still speak warmly of the way the POWs related to the whole family. That was certainly the case with the Slarke family.

> They really loved the children and the children loved them too, as toddlers always will with anyone who's nice to them. I brought a baby home from hospital and they were delighted to see the bambino, wanted to hold him.

Neville Marsh still remembers the kindness he experienced, as a small boy, from Giuseppe Varone and his cousin and fellow prisoner, Paolo. Now he sees himself as standing in for their own sons so far away in Italy. On the regular army canteen visits, when the POWs could buy razor blades and other essentials, they invariably found something for him like a few lollies, a special treat in wartime.

Naturally he took care to always be highly visible when the canteen truck drove in. He can still see Paolo and Giuseppe walking up the paddock, always in single file, to and from work, often hastening their step on canteen days.

For Irene Falconer, in the steep hills near Bridgetown, there was unexpected delight in her discovery of a musical POW duo with Carlos as tenor and Joseph as bass.

> They had two of the most beautiful voices. We had a windmill which was in the lowest part of the farm and the hills all around and they would feed the calves and we had four-gallon galvanised buckets, proper buckets, and when they'd fed the calves they would each get a bucket and hold it up and sing into it. The bucket would amplify the voice and sometimes when conditions were

right, it echoed round the hills. It was really beautiful, and they'd do that at night when they'd fed the calves.

They sang quite a lot of opera because Joseph's sister was a professional in some opera company in Italy. Carlos' favourite Australian song was Jealousy and that used to come on quite frequently. He would sit right up close to the wireless, and he would go, 'You excusa me, please? I must not miss this one,' and he'd get down and put his ear right alongside the speaker, and that was his favourite, but mostly they sang in Italian, of course, and it was the opera they loved.

However, more than any other aspect of country life in wartime Australia it was food and the preparing of meals that provided the best opportunity to exchange ideas and achieve understanding. In his free time Luigi Bassano caught

Milione de conigli. The farm was crawling with rabbits, millions of rabbits.

The POWs and Prudence Broad handled the rabbit surplus together.

Sunday was a free day and every six weeks they'd have a tea at the farm. And there'd be five or six other Italians come. And they'd make a dinner party. We'd give them whatever they needed to make their spaghetti. They would manufacture that and it was lovely, lovely spaghetti. They used to trap rabbits and cook them with the spaghetti.

In the Marsh home Giuseppe Varone and fellow prisoners taught Doreen Marsh how to make meals using spaghetti. It was not a food they had thought of eating before they acquired POWs. Using materials from the regular army canteen visits, such as tomato sauce and vermicelli, often available when spaghetti was not, they began to change the way dishes smelled and tasted.

John Bianchini, despite his name, was not a POW. However, he played a vital role in their welfare. Although he was born in Sicily, his parents had come to Australia many years before World War Two. John grew up bilingual, like many Italo-Australians of that time. In the Australian army, his skills were much in demand after the POW rural labour scheme came in. He was soon released from normal army duties to work full time as an interpreter in the country centres. It was a job he enjoyed enormously.

One of his most cherished memories was being able to settle a misunderstanding about food or, to be more accurate, a presumed lapse in table manners.

> At tea time on this particular farm they'd be feeding the POWs with them. And they'd say 'Would you like some more?' And the POW'd say 'Basta! Basta!' Anyway, this farmer said to me the day I came out, 'Look! I wish you'd tell him to stop swearing at the tea-table!' I said, 'What's he saying?' 'Oh! He keeps saying Bastard! Bastard!' I said, 'Oh, he's saying Basta! Basta! (I have enough!) I'll tell him to use another word which means the same thing.'

Irene Falconer experienced a similar problem with food and words.

> I always used to go and bring the cows in. I did it more for exercise than anything else. I'd gone out this day and the mushrooms were up and they were those nice little button ones so I picked some, and Carlos came over during the morning and he asked what was for lunch. And I showed him the mushrooms. He said, 'No, no, no.' He said, 'In Italy this one debolezza.' Well, debolezza meant that you were very debilitated or you were dead.

So he wouldn't eat it. 'All right,' I said, 'you don't get any dinner.' He said, 'You eat?' And I said, 'Yes.' So he said, 'You scribe.' So I described.

I got a piece of paper and a pencil and I had to write that I was eating mushrooms for my dinner because if I was poisoned and died he, being a prisoner of war, would be blamed. Therefore he wanted it in writing.

So 'I scribed' and he was happy and away he went, and about an hour later he came over and he said, 'You all right, Madame?' I said, 'Yes,' and he said, 'Now I eat.'

There were also special occasions. Don and Ruth Johnston had two prisoners on their Wheatbelt farm. They were not there for very long but Ruth remembers making a particular effort for one of her POWs.

I made him a birthday cake. By doing these sort of things I thought maybe somebody over there in Italy would be kind to our own men who'd been taken prisoner of war.

An English historian, Roger Absalom, conducted extensive research into the fate of Allied POWs in Italy during the 1980s. He talked with young Australians, New Zealanders and British escapees, men who escaped from POW camps after Italy's collapse in September 1943. In Italy itself, in the villages surrounding the POW camps, and in the remote mountain communities, he also spoke with Italian women who had given aid to escaped prisoners. Many expressed the same sentiments about POWs as farmers' wives in Australia. When asked why they were prepared to shelter and feed these young Australians, the reply was often, 'Maybe, somewhere, my boy, if he's captured, might need help!'

There are interesting parallels in the experience of young Australian soldiers in Italy and their Italian counterparts in Australia. The latter, for the most part, had the good fortune to fall amongst kind-hearted people, living in a country undamaged by international as well as civil war, as Italy was at this time. Where Australians were to escape into a landscape fraught with dangers, Italian prisoners had found refuge with people like the Slarke family from whom there was no need to escape.

> We did take them on a Sunday when we went to tennis. And most of the farmers around had prisoners. And they would all take them and the POWs seemed to enjoy congregating amongst themselves. They'd walk in the bush and we'd have afternoon tea and call them over to have theirs while we played tennis. And we were pleased to give them that pleasure. They enjoyed getting among the company of the other men, and being able to speak their own language of course. And they got letters from home. And I know they would take their letters with them and any photos they had and show them around.

Mick Mouritz sensed that everybody was up for assessment at those Sunday gatherings, after church or during tennis.

> We were supposed to take them into church once a month. We learnt afterwards from them (the POWs) how the other farmers were reacting to the POW business. And generally the farmers, if they didn't go to church themselves, discussed the prisoners while they were waiting.

Luigi Bassano recalls those weekends with mixed feelings.

> On Sundays we were free but there was no way we could go into town. Oh no! But on the farms we could do whatever we liked. We'd all get together, three or four of us prisoners, all get together on the farm. And who was watching us? Nobody was watching us. You could say we were workmen. And our job was to work!

Taking Bruno Anghinetti to Mass each week was one of Stephen Smith's duties. He drove Bruno to a service at a local farmhouse that served as the Catholic church. The Smith family was Church of England but Stephen reckoned the friendly Catholic priest, Father Farrelly, might convert him. He was always invited in as well. 'Don't stand outside son, come on in!' Most weeks he did, enjoying the unfamiliar hymns and form of service.

For Gwen Slarke at lonely Lake Grace, the POW presence added colour to social life in the country.

> It was a topic of conversation; our prisoners and your prisoners. And there weren't very many chances in wartime of meeting other people on a farm. There wasn't much social contact. We were glad to compare our prisoners and how they reacted to us.

Les Moriarty, of Busselton, saw out the war in the Australian army. He had been assigned to the POW scheme in the South-West. It was country he knew well, having lived there all his life. He also knew of one social contact that seemed to promise nothing but strife, at least for the POW who initiated it.

> We had one incident of a young fellow with girl trouble – the only one that I can think of, and this was on a farm at Karridale near Augusta. He was one of two prisoners on this particular farm and he suddenly got the idea into his head that he wanted a transfer, but he would never explain or never tell anybody – he was only about nineteen years old this boy – and he would never explain to the officer why he wanted a transfer.
>
> If he had a good reason for a transfer he would have got it, but he wouldn't say why it was. But a couple of miles away there was a big family and one particularly young girl that was worrying this boy a bit. He wouldn't say that was the reason that he wanted to be transferred,

> *but anyhow it eventually came that she was in the family way! The poor little devil, he thought he'd get his head chopped off! He thought that was the end of him, he'd be executed, you know. He came into our centre where we used to keep them occasionally, and we had to keep an eye on him because he might do something damned silly.*

There were similar liaisons, inevitable in the circumstances, and more frequent as the war went in the Allied favour and regulations relaxed. Local police often knew which POW had a girlfriend in town and how he got to see her. However, apart from a warning about bending the rules, the police frequently left nature well alone.

If romance might entice a POW to stray from where he was supposed to be then his conspicuous and compulsory burgundy uniform had the opposite effect. These lurid outfits were a source of both amusement and irritation to their wearers.

Ruth Johnston recalls one of their more sartorial prisoners who restyled his drab uniform into something much more dashing.

> *He was keen on making himself look smart. They were in army red-dyed uniforms. And so he asked if he could borrow my sewing machine. He made a fantastic job of smartening himself up. He looked smarter than any others.*

The idea of the burgundy outfit was to render POWs highly visible if they attempted to escape. However, for Mick Mouritz and the POWs on his Hyden farm, three hundred kilometres from the sea in any direction, the very word 'escape' became a household joke.

> *They weren't very impressed with our country. The vastness appalled them. All these miles of country. They used to say, 'Where do we escape to, Boss? You tell me and maybe I escape.'*

Bruno Anghinetti, working near Busselton on the south-west coast, was, geographically at least, in a much better position to escape than most, if he ever harboured any thoughts of freedom. He had become like a son to the Smith family and had more than made good his promise to work as hard as two men.

However, one day he had not returned from clearing at the usual time and the family became concerned. Stephen saddled up his mare and rode out to where Bruno had gone to work. He kept calling but with no reply until he heard a faint 'Over here! Over here!' He found Bruno bleeding fast from a nasty wound in the foot.

While walking along his axe had slipped from his shoulder and had almost severed a tendon. Stephen lifted him onto the mare and walked them both home. Fortunately, Stephen's mother, Margaret Smith, was a highly qualified and skilled nurse. She took one look at Bruno's foot and realised that she could treat the injury on the spot and save the tendon.

On his next visit, the District Captain wanted Bruno sent to hospital. But Margaret had cleaned the wound carefully and bound it tightly. She convinced him that good rest was all her patient needed. Bruno spent three weeks in bed but when he got up again he walked, first with two sticks but later without any trace of a limp. He made a complete recovery.

As the war went on and Italy signed an Armistice with the Allies, it became easier for both host families and POWs to bend the rules. Prisoners acquired, if unofficially, more freedom of movement. However, Luigi Bassano received a wink and a warning by the local sergeant.

> He knew us well because he used to come out to the farm on his horse. And he said to me, 'You're coming into town a bit too often. Now, you understand, I don't see you! But if anyone complains I've got to come and take you back!'

Bruno Anghinetti (centre with floppy hat) on a picnic with the Smith family.

The Mouritz family always took a break each year after harvest, going to the south coast to relax. They felt confident enough to take their POWs with them on their annual break, defying wartime regulations.

> *We couldn't see any harm in it. We took them for a fort-night's holiday down to Hopetoun on the coast. I gave them some of my clothes because if they'd been seen down there with their burgundy uniforms, there'd have been quite a furore. There were always people ready to criticise you for doing a thing like that. And they had a royal time. They were better for it and so were we. They settled down to work as soon as they got back.*

In distant Europe the struggle for the continent continued. The Allies achieved a toehold in Italy and fought their way against strong German resistance up the peninsula. This stage of the campaign was extremely worrying for Giuseppe Varone. His family lived near Cassino, the scene of intense fighting as the Allies tried to break through to the capital, Rome.

However, the war was beginning to swing against the Axis powers. With their gradual defeat and the success of the Italian partisans against the fascists, some of the early political tensions returned. One night, at the dinner table in Lake Grace, Gwen Slarke broke some important news.

> *Mussolini didn't come into their conversation at all, until we told them that he'd been killed. And one of them took that very hard. He shouted and threw his arms around. And I was really afraid then. He was having a meal with us when we told him we'd heard it on the news.*

Down in The Hollow at Bridgetown, Carlos and Joseph had obviously long planned a celebration.

> They had effigies, paper cut-outs of Mussolini and they
> had him strung up by the neck and they were hanging all
> over the place. It's a wonder the farm didn't go up in
> smoke. They would set fire to his feet and let him slowly
> burn up.

Others took news of the war and of the increasing likelihood of
Allied victory stoically, even apprehensively. When Prudence
Broad described the celebrations that would certainly mark the
return of the Australian soldiers, they told her, sadly, that no such
welcome awaited Italian POWs in their homeland. For them it was
a disgrace to have been captured in the first place.

On 30 April 1945 Adolf Hitler committed suicide beneath the
Berlin Chancellory. The Third Reich collapsed and the war in
Europe seemed at an end. Mealtime conversations in rural
Australia turned more and more towards a timetable for repatria-
tion. Mick Mouritz's POWs were impatient to be on their way.

> They thought that a couple of days after the war
> finished, they'd be going back to Italy. And it was a sore
> point with them that they were there three to four months
> after the war finished before they were taken home.

For Pasquale Amato, the end of his spell as POW came
suddenly.

> We never realised. As a matter fact, it must have been
> early in July 1946, one morning the truck came along
> with the military.
>   'Pick up everything! Hop in!' Off we went! He took
> us first to Northam and we were there for three months!

Freedom, or at least its promise, meant saying goodbye to the
Garnetts who had treated him as part of the family.

Some Italian prisoners spent their last few months in Australia working on postwar reconstruction. Arthur Moore, then with the Australian Army Pay Corps, went to a camp in Northcliffe, early in 1946, to look after pay arrangements for about a hundred and fifty Italian prisoners. He was in the last few months of his army career and this was, in his own words, a fill-in job. Within a few months the camp would be disbanded, he would be discharged and the prisoners repatriated.

The POWs were housed in a camp on an abandoned Group Settlement farm. Their last task in Australia was to help rehabilitate many of the Groupie blocks as part of a Post-War Service Land Settlement Scheme. As far as Arthur could see, the work was not strenuous and neither was the security.

> There was no security at all. There were six army people there and none of them had duties associated with keeping an eye on the prisoners. As far as I know none of us had a rifle and we took no part in any of the discipline of the prisoners. We always used to joke that the dense karri forest was the guard, and so it was.

Australia had been their prison, but some POWs refused to leave. They could see possibilities in the country that had been their gaol, and many enquired as to whether they could stay on. The authorities told them that under the Geneva Convention all prisoners of war had to be repatriated. After that it was up to them as to whether they applied to return. One or two prisoners tried to shorten that process, merging quietly into the Australian landscape, usually without success.

Repatriation was Bruno Anghinetti's sole goal when the war ended. He had not seen his family or the girl he had hoped to marry for seven years.

Stephen Smith recalls his friend's last working day as a POW. They had gone out to clear gum suckers. Bruno had packed the lunch, or some of it. But the lunch box fell out of the cart as they made their way across country to work and when they knocked off

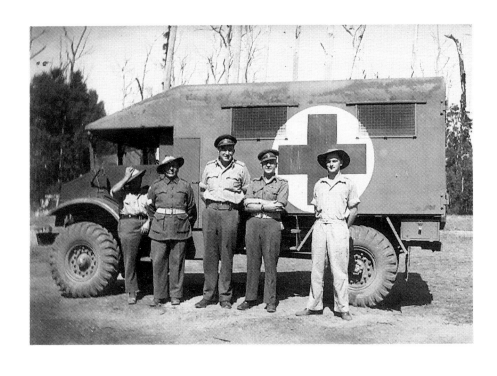

Arthur Moore (right) with army personnel at the Northcliffe prisoner of war camp.

for their midday meal there was no milk and sugar for their coffee. Bruno's mind was on other things that day.

However, it was some time before he got home. First there were five more months in Australia, spent at Northam awaiting a ship that would take him back. When he finally sailed for Naples on 4 October 1946, it was on the same vessel that had brought him from Bombay in 1943. The Smith family saw him off at Fremantle.

Late in 1946, Doreen and Arthur Marsh were also making preparations to part with Giuseppe Varone and his fellow POW.

> *I made them a fruit cake each. They were very fond of fruit cake. They weren't over the moon about going. But they were quite pleased to be on their way. But we knew we'd miss them, you know, being with us for a while.*

Giuseppe Varone was to remember Arthur Marsh's words as they prepared to leave.

> *'Look, I'm sorry you're leaving. But you must go. You've got the right to see your family too.' He said, 'You write and we'll write back.' And so we did. And then they all came to say goodbye to me at Fremantle.*

Interpreter John Bianchini knew how the POWs felt about going home.

> *I said to one chap, 'I bet you're much happier in Australia than you were in India.' And he said, 'Oh, yes, but even though we're on farms and we're fairly free, if you have a bird in a cage and you open the door he'll fly out. We're just the same. Even though we're happy, we still want to go home.' And I've never forgotten that.*

John Bianchini was to accompany many of the prisoners home.

He hadn't seen Italy himself since the age of six, so he was as chirpy as many of the POWs when the time came to embark. The voyage remained for him as one of the most moving experiences of the war.

> It was tremendous. The feeling was great. They were really excited, every day. And night-time there was music. They were all singing. A lot of chaps had made their own guitars or mandolins. Every night I'd walk around and talk to them because I knew it'd be the last time I'd be doing so. And they'd made some wonderful friends in those times.
>
> The atmosphere was electric, until we got to the Straits of Messina. And we arrived there about five o'clock. It was the end of September 1946, and I can still remember vividly. The Mediterranean was lovely and blue. And we came to the Straits and went straight through them. All of a sudden, a calm came over all the POWs. They didn't sleep all night. And neither did I because I was excited at seeing Italy again.
>
> And I said, 'But why aren't you singing tonight? There's your home town. Some of them could see the lights of their home town going past. They said, 'Oh, I live over there, in Calabria!' But they were very calm and didn't say a word. They were all silent. And it was really sad. They weren't as excited as I was. They couldn't believe that after all this time they were going home.

For John Bianchini himself, the most that he would see of Italy was a few hours on the wharf at Naples, amidst emotional family reunions, none of them his own. His aunt and uncle had set off by train from the north of Italy to see him, if only for the fortnight's leave the army had promised him. They arrived to see the repatriation vessel disappearing over the horizon, along with the nephew they would never see.

At the last moment orders had been changed by the Australian commander in Naples and the ship was ordered, with all personnel, to turn for home immediately.

For the returning POWs themselves, after the initial joy of return, postwar Italy presented a disheartening spectacle. When Luigi Bassano returned to his home town, San Vito, he found it virtually destroyed by the war.

> I saw that the whole village was razed to the ground. All the buildings were in ruins. My house was flattened. There were mines everywhere, some of them still live. Almost everything was destroyed. It made you cry, made you weep, but you had to be strong. We had to reconstruct, start all over again.

In their invasion of Italy in 1943, the Allies had concentrated their efforts on the western coast of Italy. The push towards Rome had been long, bloody and destructive. On the other side of the Apennines the Adriatic coast had also been the scene of fierce German resistance as British and American troops inched up the peninsula. Small villages like San Vito, Luigi Bassano's home, had taken the brunt.

The situation was much the same for many of his countrymen as they returned to their home towns and villages. A few began to think of Australia again. The sequels to their stories are in the postscript of this book.

Two anecdotes with which to close this chapter.

Doreen Marsh of Hyden recalls an Italian family named Della Bosca she had known before World War Two. They were then living in the small Great Southern wheat and wool town of Broomehill. Mrs Della Bosca died unexpectedly and her husband took most of the family back to Italy in the early 1930s, including the young Tommy Della Bosca, aged about six.

Some years later, in 1943, Tommy was driving a truck along a country road in north-east Italy. Ahead of him, a young man, much the same age as himself, signalled that he wanted a lift. He was an Australian POW called Jack Nelson, doing his best to look like part of the scenery. Tommy pulled up and the hitchhiker got in. They sat in silence for a while until the young Italian asked,

> 'How Broomehill?' Well, Jack nearly fell out of the truck! He must have looked amazed and then Tommy said 'You Nelson boy?' And he was.

Tommy Della Bosca had recognised one of his old Broomehill playmates. Unfortunately for young Jack Nelson, although Tommy took him as far as he could, the Germans later captured him and he became a POW for the second time.

There was a parallel incident for one Australian POW bound for Italy. After his capture by the Germans in North Africa, he and his dejected comrades waited in the hot sun at Benghazi. They were due for shipment across the Mediterranean at any time. An Italian Army truck, laden with troops bound for the North African front, halted briefly near them. From its interior he heard a voice call out in an unmistakably Australian idiom, 'Any of you blokes from Kalgoorlie?'

In the few moments before the guards moved them on, he learned that the owner of the voice, an Italian emigrant, had made a badly timed visit to Italy just before the war. As a former Italian citizen he had been immediately conscripted into the Italian army.

Unlike their Italian counterparts, Australians volunteered for their war. Nonetheless, like them, they also fought and were captured in North Africa. Italian prisoners had been sent south to Australia. Australians were to go in the opposite direction, to Italy and captivity.

LAST OF THE POW GO

● **STANDING OUT** in Gage Roads yesterday rather than berth and risk escapes, the Orontes added the last Italian prisoners of war from this State to more than 2000 Germans and Italians already on board and on their way home. This picture shows the naval embarkation launch alongside.

Australians being captured in North Africa.

MORE DANGEROUS THAN SERPENTS

Australian POWs in Italy

Well, on 27 July 1942 at Ruin Ridge, my life as a soldier had a new spectrum, I was now a Prisoner of War.

Sergeant Phil Loffman, 2/28. AIF.

I think the mothers of the Italian kids used to tell them that if they didn't behave themselves, the Australians would get them. In one propaganda article I read we were more dangerous than the serpents who hide in the grass – we were just the end of everything.

Lance Corporal Doug Le-Fevre, of the 2/28. AIF.

In the desert battles of North Africa in 1942 the Germans captured large numbers of Allied soldiers: Australians, New Zealanders and British troops. Many Australians were especially unlucky in being captured in the second battle of El Alamein. The German army handed its prisoners over to Italian army commanders who, in turn, despatched them to POW camps in Italy. Doug Le-Fevre, Phil Loffman and Jack Wauhop were just three of that number. This is the story of their imprisonment and escape, together with that of other Western Australians, Jack Hawkes, Dan Black, Jack Dodd, Jim McMahon, and John Peck from Victoria.

They were all to head out into the countryside after the Italian Armistice in September 1943 and they all came to know rural Italy and its people in a way unimaginable to most travellers in Italy today.

Their POW experiences also provide a striking contrast and some interesting parallels with those of their Italian counterparts in Australia.

Phil Loffman's first surprise was his discovery that not all Italians saw POWs as the vanquished enemy. On their arrival in Italy he and hundreds of fellow prisoners were paraded through the streets of Naples.

To his amazement, many of those who lined the streets pressed food or cigarettes into their hands. Where the captives had

Phil Loffman (left) with his horse and cart at Northam Camp.

expected taunts they found a measure of sympathy. It was a pattern that would repeat itself later when the Australian POWs escaped into the countryside after Italy's military and political collapse.

Phil was born in 1920 and had left school at fourteen. Both his parents died while he was still in his teens and he had to look after himself from an early age. At sixteen he'd already joined the militia and trained continuously, transferring into the regular army in 1939. He began war service at Northam Camp, driving a horse and cart in lieu of an armoured vehicle. Six years later, in Germany, his war would end that way.

Jack Hawkes was born in 1917 in Kalgoorlie. His father later ran a struggling grocery business in the small Wheatbelt town of Meckering.

> *The Depression came in 1929 and the farmers couldn't pay their way so poor old Dad had to keep giving food away and we couldn't pay our way. I left school the month before I was fourteen because he couldn't pay anybody to help him, so I helped Dad in the shop.*

Later he worked as a cinema projectionist until war broke out. Jack was keen to get into action. He signed up for the 2/28 Battalion in 1940 and went to Northam Camp for basic training. He'd also got married that year. A few months later, in January 1941, he was on an army embarkation train speeding non-stop through the suburbs of Perth towards Fremantle. His wife, Joyce, was looking out for him at Claremont as the train went through.

> *Every town we went through, every station we went through, they'd speed up so you couldn't see anyone. I don't know whether it was so nobody could hop off on the way through. Then when we got down to Claremont my wife was on the station and I could see her and I was*

Leaving Northam Camp for service in North Africa.

> *yelling out, 'Goodbye, goodbye, goodbye!' She was just*
> *glaring at a haze of faces going past flat out on the train.*
> *The train was going too fast.*

So would the next four and a half years. His first child, a daughter, was born while he was defending Tobruk. Jack also spent five weeks in a military hospital in Tobruk with a piece of shrapnel in his knee. It was a souvenir he would keep until doctors removed it in Australia well after the war. Waiting for admission at the hospital he saw a casualty from the other side.

> *On one of the stretchers there was an Italian and the*
> *poor bugger, that was the first time I'd seen a bayonet*
> *wound, he had it in the stomach and all of his stomach*
> *was poking out. I thought, you poor bugger. He saw me*
> *looking at him and he shut his eyes, the poor cow.*

Later, Jack transferred to a ski commando corps in Lebanon and rejoined his original unit to campaign in Libya. There, along with Phil Loffman and many others, he was taken prisoner at Ruin Ridge on 27 July 1942. Jack and his fellow prisoners travelled by diesel truck across the desert to their next destination.

> *There would have been seventy to a hundred blokes in*
> *the back and you couldn't sit down. And you had to go*
> *along these rough roads. They didn't bother about*
> *guarding you too much because there was nowhere you*
> *could go. There was all this miles and miles of desert*
> *and you had no water, you had nothing, no food or*
> *anything like that. They gave you a bit of water now and*
> *then. I mean if you thought of escaping you might as well*
> *just have gone and shot yourself – except you didn't have*
> *anything to shoot yourself with either. It was like that all*
> *the way up to Benghazi.*

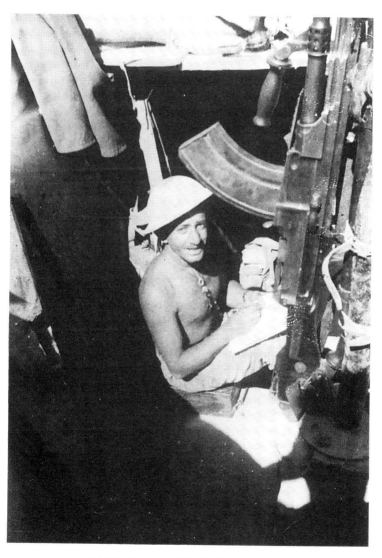

Phil Loffman in Tobruk, North Africa.

Jack was to wait In Benghazi for three months before being sent to Italy.

Dan Black was also to go to Italy the same way. He had been born in Campbelltown, Scotland, but his family came to south-western Australia as Group Settlers in the 1920's. After a few years they gave up trying to farm the heavily timbered country at Northcliffe and moved to the mining town of Collie. There both Dan and his father worked in a coalmine. Dan was sixteen when his father was killed in a mine accident, leaving him as the sole provider for his mother, sister and two brothers.

At eighteen he joined the army, partly to support his mother and family, but also in a youthful spirit of adventure and with a sense of history, transmitted by his teachers.

> One was a fellow called Ernie Durham, the best school-teacher I ever had, and he was very pro-Empire. Of course, in those days, you looked at a map and all the red was British and it was all over the world. I was brought up to that.

In April 1941 Dan Black sailed on the *Ile de France* for the Middle East. On 27 July 1942 he became a prisoner of the Germans in the second battle of El Alamein.

It was an unfortunate ending to what had been, the day before, a victory of sorts. The 2/28 had advanced rapidly some five kilometres towards their target, an outcrop called Ruin Ridge. They took the ridge without much resistance, dug in and waited for reinforcements. Unfortunately for them they were now too far ahead of their own lines. Ammunition trucks came up the next day to give them support but a German counterattack blew them up. The next day the Germans, with heavy armour, surrounded, disarmed and imprisoned the Australians.

The German army handed their captives to the Italian authorities for transfer to Italy. The Australians went en masse to the port of Benghazi. Dan has unpleasant memories of this first phase of his imprisonment at the hands of the Italian army.

We nearly starved to death. They fed us mostly on our own rations of bully beef and biscuits which they'd captured from us previously. Then I got dysentery.

Dangerously ill, he was sent across the Mediterranean, from Tripoli, on a hospital ship to the big naval base of Caserta just north of Naples. There he gradually recovered. As a convalescent, he was allowed to walk in the hospital garden. One morning he noticed a dead body being taken out of an ambulance at the hospital gates. A doctor with the ambulance summoned him over. He was told to swap places with the corpse. The ambulance took him to yet another hospital, for reasons that became clear later. This hospital, in the old Roman city of Nochera, was a fascist showplace, always available for International Red Cross inspection. Dan, as a 'recovered patient', could demonstrate its efficiency.

However, as Dan saw for himself, the death rate from dysentery was appallingly high. For all their skill, the kindly Catholic sisters who ran Nochera could not save many of the prisoners. The patients were brought into their care too late and often too weak to recover. Dan was offered fresh fruit rejected by men too ill to swallow food. It accelerated his own recovery.

At Nochera hospital he also met another survivor of Ruin Ridge, his own lieutenant. This officer had been badly wounded and had also lost one eye. He was awaiting repatriation to Australia by the Red Cross. Under the League of Nations, repatriation, in the middle of war, was allowed where soldiers were obviously unfit for future combat.

When he returned to Australia the lieutenant contacted Dan's mother and was able to tell her that he had last seen her son, alive and well in Nochera.

However, Dan was soon to move again, this time to the other

side of Italy, to Cividale and POW Camp 57, Gruppignano, where he rejoined many of his former comrades from the 2/28 Battalion.

One of the most unusual figures in this story is John Peck, from Crib Point in Victoria. Peck was born in Woollahra, Sydney, in 1922, but his father, a serving officer in the Royal Australian Navy, was transferred to Victoria and John Peck grew up at Crib Point. When he left school, he joined droving teams and worked largely in the company of older men. He was seventeen when the war came but put his age up to twenty-one. World War Two was to be his big adventure.

He spent the first year fighting in Libya, but in May 1941 his unit went to Greece. The Germans, having conquered much of the Greek peninsula, were determined to secure Crete in order to counter British naval dominance in the Mediterranean. The Luftwaffe dropped wave after wave of paratroopers onto the island and heavily bombed Allied airfields and the British naval base at Suda Bay. Initially, the British, Australian and New Zealand troops repelled the attacks but were overwhelmed by superior German air power. The order was given to evacuate Crete to save Allied lives. The Luftwaffe made this operation difficult too. They destroyed four British naval ships carrying troops away from the island. So it was in Crete that John Peck became a prisoner for the first time.

> *I was captured at a place called Sfakia when the Royal Navy could no longer pick up further troops because there were tremendous losses. There I was captured and, with my small group of friends in the army, very quickly broke out of the net because being the rearguard we'd seen on the way across from Canea and Suda Bay and Galatos, on the other side of the island, that the area from one side to the other was devastated and had no food, and particularly no water whatsoever; and it would be a terrible journey back if you were being herded back*

100

as a prisoner because the roads were few and far
between, and everyone would have to walk.

The battle for Crete had been a desperate holding operation,
fought with great courage by the Australians and New Zealanders
but against overwhelming odds.

> Some of our comrades had managed to get away in a
> little rowing boat and I gave one group of our Company
> people a small Union Jack, which I'd taken from a dead
> body of a British officer in Greece, and I gave them this
> to wave in case aircraft went over that were allied
> aircraft, or even submarines or ships, that could identify
> them. They eventually sailed into Alexandria harbour
> and that flag is now in the Australian War Memorial in
> Canberra.

Peck's first escape proved easier than most of his subsequent
attempts.

> We were captured en masse but we eventually got away
> because there were just not enough German troops to
> round up thousands and thousands and thousands of
> prisoners. So, after a few days, we got away and we made
> our way back over the mountains to a place called
> Gorgiopolous where we had been stationed for the
> invasion of Crete. We knew people there, the Cretans,
> who would help us and they did. We stopped there until
> some two months later when I was eventually singly
> captured by the Germans and taken to Canea in Crete.
>   This involved no privations except thirty days in
> gaol in supposedly solitary confinement which all prison-
> ers throughout the world do when they escape. This is the
> standard world punishment for it (you know, due to
> Geneva Conventions) and it is usually done in a civilian

*prison because they have very little facilities for solitary
confinement in a prison camp. When I'd done the thirty
days and gone back to Galatos prison camp I escaped ten
days later and went back to join my comrades whom I'd
left at Gorgiopolous.*

*When I got back there they had disappeared, and
thereafter, I was on my own until I met a New Zealand
soldier called Noel Dunne. We joined up together for the
rest of our time in Crete.*

Peck and Dunne made contact with many other escaped prisoners and never-captured soldiers, troops who had hidden out ever
since the German invasion. By this time the British had organised
a plan for their rescue. Under cover of darkness, surface vessels
and submarines came close to the less well patrolled southern
coast of Crete and took men off at planned intervals.
Unfortunately for John Peck, when word came through, just before
Christmas 1941, that another rescue operation was due, he was
severely ill with malaria. The boat duly came. Many got away but
he was left, along with other sick and wounded men. They were
all living hand-to-mouth at this time, dependent on the silence of
the Cretan partisans and the food they and their families provided
whenever they could.

*So I then went further to the west and eventually got into
the Italian part where Noel Dunne and I had found
some radio transmitting sets dropped by British aircraft
up in the mountains, and we were in a shepherd's hut
trying to make these sets work when an Italian patrol
grabbed us and we were then back in the bag again.*

This time Peck was sent to Rhodes. In April 1942 he and Noel
Dunne escaped again. They were recaptured and put in a civilian
gaol, and later in a prison camp in the centre of the island. John
Peck broke out of that prison too, and with Noel Dunne and a few

companions, stole a boat and set off for Turkey not far across the Aegean.

> We escaped with three Czech prisoners, who unfortu-
> nately didn't survive the boat trip to Turkey – Noel
> Dunne and I did. We were picked up by an Italian
> destroyer and taken back to Rhodes, but unfortunately
> the others were drowned. The boat had sunk in a storm
> which quickly blew up and the timbers were rotten – it
> was only a small boat.

He had by now escaped four times from German or Italian compounds.

> If you're young, agile and foolish, you do things that
> older wiser men never do, and mostly you get away with
> it. Mostly you don't think of any consequence because
> you've got no children or wife to worry about, you've got
> no position of authority to maintain, you're you and you
> take your chance, and the quicker you take it the better
> off you'll be.

This time the Germans were determined not let Peck out of their sight. They held him for a while in Greece but finally handed him over to the Italian army. Peck arrived in Bari in southern Italy in May 1942, and shortly afterwards was sent to Udine, in northeast Italy, almost on the Yugoslav border. There he rejoined fellow Australians and, later, helped many of them escape.

Peck's time on the run was soon to come in handy. In Crete he'd quickly learnt Greek and had discovered a natural aptitude for languages. Now he learnt Italian from the prison guards.

> They were very pleased when somebody tried to learn
> their language and they really went out of their way to
> help you. You also had, in these prison camps, very many

well-educated prisoners who to relieve their boredom anyway, were quite happy and willing to teach every subject under the sun, including Italian.

Jim McMahon, like John Peck, was also to learn Italian but his route to Italy was very different. He was born in 1915 at Lake Yealering in wheatbelt Western Australia, the youngest of six children. When he was two-years-old his mother left home. His father promptly rode to the nearest large town, Narrogin, and asked the police to pick up his children and put them into orphanages. His two brothers went to the Christian Brothers' orphanage at Clontarf on the Canning River, then well beyond the boundaries of Perth. Jim joined them in 1919 and did a few years schooling. However, at Clontarf, classes ended at Grade Seven. From now on he was expected to earn his bed and board. Jim milked cows, chopped wood and worked in the orphanage garden.

In 1928, the brothers sent him to their new farm school at Tardun, east of Geraldton. At thirteen he was the smallest and youngest worker and got all the chore jobs. Accommodation was rough. The three Christian Brothers and six boys slept in bough huts, their sides cut from the surrounding bush. Even this housing proved short-lived. One day, when Jim was lighting the laundry copper, a willy-willy raced through the settlement, the flames fanned and ate up the bush walls next to the laundry. Within ten minutes the bough huts were grey rectangles of ash. It fell to Jim to tell the boss, Brother Keaney, what had happened. He saddled the farm pony and rode off to find him.

> *'Couldn't you save anything?' Brother Keaney demanded.*
> *'No, it was all too quick!'*
> *'Well, what's left?'*
> *'Only what you're standing in, Brother, and what I'm standing in.'*

At sixteen he had to fend for himself. He worked in a variety of jobs, including dairy work at Wiluna and shearing on North-West stations. By 1938 Jim was working at Reedy's mine in the Murchison goldfields near Cue. He had to queue for the job, along with hundreds of others, and was lucky to get work.

A year later the army sent a recruiting officer to the Goldfields in search of volunteers. The prospect of a soldier's life interested Jim but he was earning good money for the first time in his life; working on the lower levels and being rewarded for the risk. Older men, who'd seen World War One from the Western Front in France, warned him not to go. They told him about life in the trenches and the appalling casualty rates but, in the end, their memories didn't put him off.

Early in January 1941, Private Jim McMahon of the 2/28 Battalion left Fremantle on the *Aquitania*, bound for the Middle East. The last section of the battalion left the *Aquitania* in Ceylon (now Sri Lanka) and made the final part of the journey in smaller boats.

Jim was to see action first at the siege of Tobruk where Australians held the German army off for two hundred and fourteen days. Later he was to campaign in Syria with the Ski Corps for several months. At this point he thought his war might be over. The troops had been promised a fortnight's leave and then passage to Australia. Events had changed rapidly in the North African campaign. They were hurriedly recalled and sent into action at the second battle of El Alamein on 27 July 1942.

German scouts were coming up and we were getting rid of all our ammunition, firing off at them. Then I suddenly heard some noise coming from behind us and I thought it was our tanks coming. We were lying in our sangers with our heads down towards the ground you see, and I had my tin hat on and I saw this tank come over the rise, or the armoured car it was really, and then it swung around side-on and I said, 'It's the flaming Germans.' I thought they were ours coming. Next thing,

which I didn't know at the time, a bullet hit me right in
the middle of the forehead, went over the top off my head
and out the back of my tin hat and left a hole as big as
you could put your fist through. When I came to I said
to the chaps alongside of me, I said, 'I'm dead!' I thought
I was. They said to me afterwards that it threw me about
ten feet in the air.

When I came to I was flat on my back. I put my
hand up to my head, I looked at my tin hat. The bullet
must have killed me surely. I came away with a handful
of bloody hair. Next thing I knew a German officer was
standing near and saying, 'Oop.' Of course, I didn't get
up straightaway and he turned around and walked back
towards his vehicle. When he left to go back to his
vehicle I picked up my tin hat and I walked out with the
others. Then I walked right up to him and the nearer I
got to him, the whiter he went. When I got right up to
him as close as I am to you he said, 'You're dead.' 'No,
I'm not dead,' I said, 'your German bullets are not good
enough to kill me.' Anyway he said, 'You go past a
dressing station on your way back to the prison camp and
you can get a dressing put on it, make sure dust doesn't
get into it.' 'Good God,' I said, 'one minute you're trying
to murder me and the next minute you're trying to save
my life.' He said, 'Oh well, that's what we're here for.'

I was taken prisoner on the 28th of July at about
11.00 am the morning after we'd gone into action. We
thought we were the only ones that had been taken until
we got to the prison camp and the rest were there.

Jim and his fellow prisoners travelled back to Tobruk, now in
German hands, and two days later were trucked to Benghazi. In
Benghazi, the Australians were told they were to be sent on to Italian
prison camps. Still hoping to escape, they tried to delay the inevitable.

*We were put in this prison camp there and they gave us
nothing to lie on, only just the ground sheet. Of course,
they wanted to get the Australians out of there as quick
as they could and across to Italy you see. But half-a-
dozen of us were good mates, we'd crawled from under
barbed wire into another compound where there were different nationalities, and we'd say to them, 'If you want to
go to Italy you can go, we'll change names with you.' So
we were there right up until about some time in the
middle of October and by this time our clothes were worn
out. We had no clothes, only what we tried to put
together out of the Eyetie groundsheets.*

They were then to cross the Mediterranean with only two days'
rations per prisoner. They'd been told it would only be only a
forty-eight-hour journey across to Taranto, at the foot of Italy, but
British destroyers patrolled the sea north to south. So the journey
turned into a Mediterranean cruise, taking in almost every island
between Italy and Greece. They finally disembarked at Taranto in
southern Italy.

*We were pretty hungry by the time we got to Italy. And
the first thing they did was take my flaming tin hat and
chuck it in the Mediterranean. I was going to try and
bring it home as a souvenir. Then they gave us an Eyetie
uniform to put on, and they put us through this blooming
steamer they had because there were lice still on us, the
eggs and everything. We never had a decent wash all that
time. They put us through this steamer and all the
steamer did was hatch out all the other blessed eggs we
had. We were lousy with lice. Then they took us from
Taranto to a prison camp at Bari.*

Jack Dodd had joined the 2/28 Battalion in 1939. He came from a
farming family at Boyup Brook. For Jack school was simply a

holding paddock. The day he left he helped drove a hundred head of cattle to the coast at Capel. When he wasn't working on the land he was ballroom dancing. So when his dancing pals, one by one, left the dance floor for the parade ground, Jack followed, aged eighteen. He knew he wouldn't get his parents' consent to join the army so he put his age up to twenty-four. He, too, was taken at Ruin Ridge and sent to Benghazi.

> It was a funny kind of feeling. I'd imagined being in the front line or perhaps being killed or losing an arm or a leg. But the idea of being a prisoner never entered my mind.

On 12 November Jack Hawkes, Jack Dodd, Phil Loffman and many other POWs left Benghazi for Italy. The Allies recaptured the port four days later.

If they'd just missed liberation, they were lucky, as Jack Dodd realised at the time, to have made it safely to Italy. From England Churchill had issued an order to sink all Italian shipping, naval or merchant marine. The other POW ship in their convoy across the Mediterranean, the *Nino Bixio*, was torpedoed by a Royal Navy submarine operating from Malta. Hundreds of Allied POWs and Italian crewmen were drowned.

For Jack Hawkes their own voyage was no pleasure cruise but it had some compensations.

> We were in the rear hold of the ship and I suppose there must have been four or five hundred POWs down there. There wasn't enough room for everybody to lie down. I was one of the first down and I saw a case that looked like food. Several of us rushed across to this case and got the lid off it and found out it was full of tins. We didn't know what they were. Any rate we found out they were tins of peas, and we hadn't had anything to eat for ages. I forget how we got them open but we got stuck straight into them.
>
> And then we found out that underneath us was

another hold, and underneath that hold there were lots of cases of all sorts of stuff and a lot of parcels with German clothes. As a matter of fact one bloke found a German officer's uniform and the silly bugger put it on.

Anyway we were in this blooming hold and we were getting all sorts of food, and we got caraway seed biscuits, tins of liverwurst – and they were great big kilo tins of them; tins of all sorts of stuff. We were just eating these tins non-stop.

Then it started. We started to get sick. We vomited a lot and still ate more, and we started to get diarrhoea and we still ate.

More than halfway through the circuitous route to southern Italy, the guards began to suspect that their charges were living on more than the statutory daily biscuit and tin of bully beef.

In the middle of the Corinth Canal they stopped the ship, put us ashore, sent their own men down to clean up the hold where we'd been and told us, 'Any man that goes into that lower hold again will be shot.' So they loaded us on again and there were some poor blokes up in the hold at the other end of the ship, they hadn't got to any tins like we had. It was incredible how those poor sods didn't get any food at all and we'd been stuffing ourselves, and vomiting it up again and again. And we had to go onto the top deck to go to the latrines and you were only allowed up one or two at a time. They were frightened of being overpowered I think.

Eventually the POWs disembarked at Brindisi. The thing Jack Hawkes wanted most was a shave.

We'd been in prison from July to November so we were all bearded. You used to borrow scissors to cut around your mouth so you could eat. Everybody was bearded so they took us to this Italian delousing station. We had lice everywhere! Wicked things to have and you get them underneath your arms, and you get them over all your body but not on your beard, strangely enough, or in your head hair, but all your body hair – lice! And you got these bloody things all the time. As well as lice you got fleas, and you had lice eggs everyday.

Anyway they got us to this delousing station and first thing the barber just got you with the clippers and he just went straight up under your chin, right up over the top of your head and over the top, and you finished up a bald-headed bloke.

And we'd got thin. When I'd been in that commando ski unit I got to over twelve stone, and when we got to Italy and went out on a working job, I was round about seven stone. We were skinny fellows, by God we were!

By taking on outside work as a carpenter, Jack Hawkes was able to obtain extra rations, mostly macaroni, which gave him a temporary fat belly but didn't do much else for him. Variety came from elsewhere.

Oh we used to get English food parcels and New Zealand and Australian, but there weren't enough for everybody, so we used to get one food parcel for fourteen blokes. There was supposed to be one food parcel per bloke per week – or sometimes it was per fortnight. So you used to whack everything up. They used to have a little pack of sultanas in every parcel, so every sultana was counted out, one for you, one for me and you never got a lot.

That was tough there and, of course, a lot of blokes died down there, and Victor Emmanuel, the King, he gave us, for a Christmas present, an orange about that

110

big, and I was that bloody hungry I ate the lot, skin and
all, and spewed it all up again!

However, apart from short rations, Jack felt that his first Italian
POW camp wasn't too bad.

We did almost what we liked. We had to be counted
once a day on the parade ground. You used to stand out
there. They were terrible counters, the Italians. There
were three thousand or so prisoners, and it used to take
them three or four hours to count us so we'd be out there
for ages.

Jack and his fellow prisoners had been kept in holding camps
near Brindisi, on the south-east toe of the Italian peninsula. On 10
July 1943 the Allies began the invasion of Sicily. The Italian army
began to move its prisoners north. They made a long railway
journey up the Adriatic coast towards Camp 57, Gruppignano,
under the command of Commandant Calcatera.

Camp 57 was sited at Udine, in north-east Italy, not far from
the Yugoslav border. The first surprise for many Australian POWs
was finding so many other nationalities behind the same wire,
New Zealanders, British, Poles, Canadians, Indians and South
Africans, as well as Serbs and Polish soldiers.

Reactions to camp life varied. Some found the discipline harsh
and petty. For others boredom became their chief enemy. POWs
could, however, have the full run of the compound, so Jack Dodd
passed the time in frequent visits to different parts of the camp to
see friends. On one tour he and his mates found an empty hut
and planned to move in. However, other prisoners warned him
that this building was a 'no go' area.

They'd already started digging an escape tunnel and they
had to reveal what they'd done. They told us we
wouldn't be able to take part but they had to tell us

Italian propaganda postcard.

because they were digging there.

It was an amazing tunnel, one hundred and thirty-four feet long – they'd dug it with knives and forks. They'd made bellows out of Red Cross tins and were pumping air down to the fellows digging. Some of them passed out down there and they had to go down and pull them out of the tunnel.

But they kept going and going and there was a crop of maize just outside the wire. And they planned the tunnel to come up in the middle of that maize crop. But it took so long that it was wintertime when the tunnel was finished and just before they were ready to break out, the nearby farmer came and cut the maize.

And then it rained and rained and the rain washed the end in and you could see a hole in the ground. You could see it from the sentry box – we could see it from the hut. We couldn't do anything about it until that night when they crawled out and boarded the hole up.

Eventually eighteen men got away through the tunnel but none lasted more than two days in the bleak north Italian countryside. Winter had set in, rivers were in flood and travel was almost impossible. However, these POWs had confounded the camp commandant, Commandant Calcatera, who had boasted that no one would escape from Gruppignano.

After a spell in Bari, southern Italy, in the late summer of 1943, Jim McMahon was sent north to a similar camp, PG 59 near Servigiliano, in Central Italy on the Adriatic side of the Apennines. There it seemed his fellow countrymen had also earned their reputation as 'diggers'.

About the second morning after we were there this commandant told us on parade, 'Last time Australians were

113

here,' he said, 'they tried to escape. They dug a tunnel out and some of them got away but we recaptured them. What you have got to do,' he said, 'is take the slat beds out of the hut every day and take the floorboards up so that we can see that there are no tunnels. The ones that have cement slabs on the floor, we want taken out too. We'll come around and tap all the slabs and make sure there's no hollow sounds.'

Underground escape from PG 59 was obviously out of the question. Undeterred, the new crop of Australians racked their brains for another way of getting out. They were still working out how to make and hide an escape ladder when Italy declared an armistice in September 1943.

Jack Wauhop's soldiering career came to an abrupt halt at Gruppignano. He had joined the 2/32 Battalion in 1940, putting his age up to get in. The eldest of five children, at fourteen Jack began work on a variety of farms in the South-West and the Wheatbelt.

It was Depression time, the wages were low, seven shillings and sixpence a week, and the work was hard. At night he lay in grain sheds where snakes hunted mice around his bed and sometimes on it. In Bridgetown he slept surrounded by the sight and smell of apples, stored in their racks. Later he took to riding the trains in the Wheatbelt, where at least the work and the pay were better, even if the tasks were just as hard.

Awful jobs but good training for the army.

It was seasonal work for the most part, driving horses, fallowing, shearing, but he was nearly always in work. At Ballidu, in the northern Wheatbelt, the farmer for whom he was fallowing, provided bread, marmite and black tea for breakfast — there was no cow to milk — served black tea, bread and marmite for lunch

114

and trotted out the same fare for the evening meal. It was not easy to question this gastronomic preference.

Don't you like marmite?

After a week of this 'grim repetition', Jack offered to go and shoot a rabbit. The employer took part of the hint. From now on rabbits and black tea made up the daily menu.

In 1939, in the Wheatbelt town of Wyalkatchem, an earnest patriot had ploughed up the local footy ground for wartime food production. It was then that Jack knew someone was taking the idea of war seriously.

If the war is going to start in Wyalkatchem then I'd better be in it.

Taken prisoner in North Africa, Jack went to Benghazi with many of his compatriots. He was aware of his POW status from the moment he reached his first Italian holding camp, at Taranto. There he was made to change into prisoner of war uniform and then sent out into the compound.

> *There was a very high fence around it, lined by Italian women all dressed in black, all crying, gesticulating towards us and muttering to themselves in a foreign language which we didn't know a word of, and I got the impression that they were expressing some sympathy for us – until a nearby guard, speaking in perfect English, said, 'They're not crying for you, mate. They're looking at you as killers of their menfolk in North Africa who are not coming back. They're pointing the finger at you now.' And that made me realise I was a prisoner of war in a hostile environment.*

115

Soon, however, he was sent north, to Camp 57, Gruppignano. This camp confirmed Jack's apprehensions about prison life.

> We had midnight parades – barefoot on frozen ground – just to be counted. They'd count two or three huts, a hundred and twenty men at a time. You weren't given any time to get dressed. You were just moved out at the point of a bayonet. It took them about an hour to count you. They wanted to check every detail, couldn't believe you were who you said you were. And then ten minutes later when you'd gone back it was all out again!

Jack Wauhop was never one to accept what he considered arbitrary or unjustified treatment. For a minor misdemeanour, failure to salute an officer, he was made to stand on parade until his legs could take no more. Today he is still paying for his defiance. Blows on the back with a rifle butt left him with injuries that have worsened with age. The man who ordered them, Camp Commandant Calcatera, was later executed for war crimes by the Allies.

For Jack Hawkes, Gruppignano's harsh discipline also came as a shock.

> We wondered what we'd struck! We had to salute officers and stand at attention if an officer went past, even a blooming sergeant, and they used to come and search your place. The blokes were getting seven days and twenty-eight days for not doing this and not doing that.

One and all, the prisoners complained about the food, though, as an Italian officer told Jack Dodd, it was what the Italian guards had to eat themselves. Jack and others became ingenious at making the best of it.

> And the real meal that I think kept us alive was the night meal where we'd get a dixie full of stewed-up vegeta-

*bles, and it was all the offcuts of what the Italians
would have. You never got a cauliflower, you always got
the stalks. Big hunks of horseradish, and we used to say
we've given better stuff to the pigs. And so we had, but I
really believe that was one of the most valuable meals we
had in the camp because it was the outside leaves of the
vegetables, it was the greens. We'd drink the water off it.
Some of the guys were disgusted with it and wouldn't
drink the water but I had every bit that I could get and
someone else's too. And I've thought over it since and I
believe that was the best meal we could get even though it
did look like pig slops.*

Jack Wauhop developed a craving for both sugar and salt.

*You'd go for weeks at a time thinking of nothing but
being back in Melbourne or Sydney or Hobart, dunking
chocolate biscuit pieces into a tin of condensed milk.
That phase would pass. The next thing you would love
to lick a horse that'd been working in the plough all day.
Lick that lather off it. That was the salt craving. Sugar
and salt.*

Jack probably had more time for daydream cravings than most
of his fellow POWs. For his 'misdemeanour' he'd been denied the
prisoner's right to write letters home through the Red Cross.

Anzac Day 1943 was to bring relief from harsh discipline, bad
food and boredom. Jack Wauhop and two hundred other
Australian POWs were to leave Gruppignano. They were sent by
train westwards across northern Italy to the town of Vercelli,
which lay between Turin and Milan and not far from the French
border. The Italian government needed labour in the rice fields.
Dan Black felt it was the best thing that had happened since he
had become a POW.

*Because there they really tried to look after us. They
found out we were pretty good workers, and the Italian
farmers used to give us extra rations, or slip us half-a-
dozen eggs and things like that.*

This move was more than just a break in routine, it provided
the beginning of contact with the Italian country people, and it
nourished thoughts of escape in the Australians.

Doug Le-Fevre was one of those sent to Vercelli. He was only ten
when he arrived in Western Australia from England in 1928.
Like Phil Loffman, he had to fend for himself early in life. In
1935 he was working on a farm in the midlands district near
Walebing. So was Eileen Jones. She was a governess to a farming
family in the district. Once in a while, Doug drove a horse and
cart over to this particular farm to pick up food for his boss'
pigs. Eileen's first sight of Doug was when a strong brown arm
appeared at the kitchen window. She admired the arm and later
came to know the owner. Doug volunteered to collect pig food
more often and stayed to play snakes and ladders with the governess.

Five years later, in September 1940, they married. He had
already joined the Light Horse at Cunderdin and later the 2/28
Battalion. Friends wondered if they'd ever join the knot. The
marriage had been postponed twice, when Eileen developed, in
succession, an abscess on her tooth and then German measles. At
the third try, Doug showed up looking green from the effects of
pre-embarkation needles. This time, however, they made it to the
altar. Three months later Doug was posted overseas.

In the second battle of El Alamein, on 27 July 1942 when the
2/28 Battalion advanced to occupy Ruin Ridge, Doug joined many
other prisoners and was shipped to Brindisi in southern Italy. He
had been badly wounded in the upper arm and spent six months
in three different hospitals. At first the Italian doctors wanted to
amputate but Doug resisted strongly. After all, this arm had an

Australian wounded being carried through the barbed wire perimeter fence,. Tobruk, North Africa.

admirer back in Australia. Finally, at Bergamo hospital, north of Milan, he recovered.

During convalescence he had also picked up a working knowledge of Italian. His teacher was one of Mussolini's political prisoners. Doug continued to improve his new language during the next twelve months. It was an effort that would reward him later.

Discharged from hospital, he too was sent to Camp 57, Gruppignano, a gaol he was more than glad to exchange for labour in the Vercelli rice country. At their work camp at Ronseca Doug worked in the rice fields by day, played games of bridge with Dan Black at night, and began to harbour thoughts of escape.

There was an obvious benefit in getting away from Commandant Calcatera and the rigidity of Camp 57. There was also a chance of revenge of sorts. Farm work provided excellent opportunities for sabotage. Doug made systematic attempts to wreck a sturdy British-made rice thresher by dropping large stones into its innards. However, the machine managed to digest these offerings with apparent ease. Rice sacks destined for Germany often reached their required weight with generous supplements from pebbles and other unmentionable detritus from the North Italian landscape. Nobody knows to this day how this affected the Nazi war effort but it afforded malicious delight to both Doug Le-Fevre and Jack Wauhop.

Their experience in the work parties also provided them with fresh air and better food. There was little meat, just the occasional piece of horseflesh, but the authorities supplied bags of macaroni and rice, and the Australian POW camp cook made the best of what he was given. There were no rabbits to go with spaghetti but overall the diet was a distinct improvement on the watery gruel of Gruppignano.

As the prisoners became friendly with local Italians, the occasional chook made its way onto the menu. Fish was also sometimes available after the rice harvest. After cropping the farmers flooded their rice fields and stocked them with carp, bony fish, as Jack Dodd recalls, but a very welcome addition to the diet of men doing hard work in the fields all day.

In Dan Black's POW quarters, the Italian lieutenant in charge of prisoners stopped one day to taste the 'risotti' his prisoners were preparing. 'How the hell do you eat this?' he asked. He was so appalled at the Australian way of cooking rice that he deputed one of the Italian army cooks to provide it for them. There were no complaints.

Accommodation also improved. Unlike Italian POWs in Australia, who lived on farms and often slept in the homestead, Australian prisoners slept in double-storey billets away from the main farmhouse.

They were also, for the first time, meeting Italians in natural circumstances. People from the Udine region and city dwellers or Mondinis as they were known (in many ways the equivalent of the Australian Land Army), toiled alongside the Australian POWs.

At Ronseca they also slept alongside the Australians, separated only by a thin wall. Jack Dodd recalls a minor panic one night when a couple of POWs drove nails into a wall so that they could hang up their clothes. It was so thin that the nails went right through and out on the other side.

The young Mondini women thought this was an attempted breakthrough by lust-crazed Australian demons. However, as Doug Le-Fevre recalls, they soon realised that Australians were not the creatures of fascist propaganda. As companionship grew, the talk that flowed from it helped break down barriers created by ignorance and isolation.

> From what they had heard, Australia and Britain and everybody had had it and when we get there, we're reasonably clothed, we're happy and we're bright. We're full of jokes. We lay down the law. We assert our authority. We don't really know who are the prisoners, them or us. They had the bright idea of putting one civilian with each POW, and the idea was we'd work as hard as the

May the Lord grant His Christmas peace to the prisoners of war of every nation whom adversity has made doubly dear to Us. The longer and more painful the separation from their country and their dear ones, the deeper be this peace within their hearts. At this holy season of Christmas Our prayers for them are still more fervent, and on them and on their families We call down God's choicest blessings.

Pius PP. XII

Page from book given by Pope Pius XII to all prisoners of war, Christmas 1942.

civilians. And of course we'd tell them what Australia
was like, and this was surprising to them, because as one
man said, they thought it was all alfalfa, lucerne.

At the Ronseca work camp thirty men slept upstairs and thirty
below. Italian soldiers guarded the building and accompanied the
POWs to work in the fields each day. To Jack Dodd the security
seemed very lax.

> *We'd have a guard go out with us each day when we*
> *went out to work. He'd have a sleep under the tree. And*
> *so the guys one day had a bit of a joke on him while he*
> *was asleep. They went and pulled the bolt out of his*
> *rifle. And the panic that came over that poor guy when*
> *he woke up. I think the authorities'd have shot him if*
> *they'd known. But we gave it back to him before he got*
> *home.*

Such opportunities encouraged thoughts of escape, and unlike
their Italian counterparts in the vast empty spaces of Australia, the
Australians in Italy had somewhere to escape to and a motive for
getting away.

123

Australian and New Zealand POWs in a northern Italian camp.

TIME TO GO

Escape — with the Partisans — return to Australia

I'd already done a dummy run, a couple of months before into Switzerland. So I knew the routes. I then started an organisation to get POWs out of Italy and made arrangements for people to pick up and guide the prisoners after I'd started organising back on the plains.

John Peck, POW escape organiser.

There was a guy who was doing a bit of organising. And I haven't heard of the man since. And it came to my mind the other day. We talk about Peck's fishpaste. This guy's name was Johnny Peck. I never knew him, only saw him briefly when he came into the train that was going up to Switzerland. I don't really know who he was.

Jack Dodd, one of many POWs to benefit from John Peck's escape network.

For Australian prisoners of war, now free of the compound and the barbed wire, life had improved in the open country of the north Italian plain. Working in the rice fields they had eaten better and had become fitter. Working alongside locals, their knowledge of the Italian language and landscape improved. During the daytime they were only lightly guarded and it was tempting to imagine, if not actually plan, a getaway. Their nearest hope lay in neutral Switzerland. That journey meant crossing the formidable snow-covered Italian Alps.

Jack Wauhop took a chance one morning, when their guard had momentarily turned his back, to escape across the rice fields. With scarcely a word of Italian he felt unable to trust himself with the local population. He hid by day and travelled at night, living off the country, eating root vegetables from the fields and occasionally raiding a farm for food. He reached the Swiss border in just a few weeks.

John Peck had continued to master the Italian language and he also made it to Switzerland this way.

> We decided, because I was the only one who spoke Italian, that we would try to get to Switzerland without coming into contact with any Italians whatsoever. And so

we started off through the foothills of the Alps and then
the Alps and we actually got into Switzerland. And you
look into Switzerland and all you see is range after range
of these high, snow-covered mountains. And never having
been there before, the feeling is you were going to die in
there. There's nothing there, no people, no animals. We
had just passed through this valley so we knew there were
people there. We said, 'Let's find a shepherd and see if
we can get some food.' So we went back into Italy and
duly found a shepherd lower down the mountain. He
promised us food and he came back after dark but with
the army and the police. And so we were recaptured.

But not for long. In the chaos that followed Italy's withdrawal
from the war in September 1943, looters raided the Vercelli gaol
where John Peck had been held and freed him. Again Peck headed
for Switzerland.

I'd already done a dummy run, a couple of months
before. So I knew the routes. I knew all the areas involved
and what to avoid and things like that and, by and large,
those Italians who weren't on our side, or sympathetic,
they were neutral. So I then decided to make for
Switzerland and got up halfway when I had pangs of
conscience and decided that for me to go in to
Switzerland and freedom meant now abandoning all my
friends, who had no way of knowing which way to go and
how to get there.
    So I decided to go back and get these people and
take them into Switzerland. I started off an organisation
with the Italians and made arrangements on the route for
people to pick up and guide the prisoners after I'd started
organising back on the plains.

His decision was shortly to make all the difference to Jack Dodd

John Peck (left) with Oreste Ferrari who was responsible for arranging guides to take prisoners of war to the Swiss border.

and Doug Le-Fevre. The Peck network was to bring over six hundred Allied POWs safely across the Swiss border.

Escape for prisoners of war in Italy had become a necessity rather than an option. Almost without warning, on 8 September 1943, the head of the Italian government, Marshal Badoglio, offered unconditional surrender to the Allied forces under General Eisenhower. The king of Italy, Victor Emmanuel, and the Grand Council had already secretly arrested and deposed Il Duce, Benito Mussolini on 25 July. From now on Italian forces would work with the Allies to expel the German army from the peninsula, a task that would prove far from easy. Italy was now in a state of civil war, as Communist partisans fought against fascists, or Republicans as they called themselves, still loyal to their deposed chief, Mussolini. The German army was still everywhere, especially in the north, at full strength and determined to recapture and deport any escaped POWs to their factories and work camps in Austria and Germany.

Phil Loffman, then in a rural POW camp, near Vercelli, heard the news of Italy's surrender from the Italians themselves.

The chappie we had as a lieutenant lined us all up and he said, 'La Guerra e finita. The War is finished!' He said that he was pro-British and when the British arrived here none of his guards should shoot at them. He, himself, was going with his wife and family that night to Switzerland. The last I saw of him was pedalling his bicycle down the road. Before he went he suggested that the guards could do as they pleased. They could stay here and guard the prisoners but it was up to them and he said to us, 'Sergeant. It's your parade and as for you prisoners, good luck!' So, we had a bit of a ball. Some went, some stayed. We had a kind of a garage sale in the camp. All the civvies came round. We sold the kitchen utensils. We sold everything we could lay our hands on for our escape money, got a few bob in our pockets, changed our uniforms into civvy clothes and the big adventure was on!

129

The Allied advance up the Italian peninsula was still slow and painful. All through the last months of 1943, stubborn German resistance and counterattack slowed up British and American progress towards the capital, Rome. On 13 November, US General Marcus Clark held a grim talk with his British colleague, Sir Harold Alexander. Both men agreed that further attempts to advance northwards would lead to costly and pointless sacrifice of both British and American lives.

For POWs in the north of Italy, two routes now lay open. They could try to go south and rejoin their own troops or they could attempt the shorter but still difficult journey across the Alps into Switzerland. The southern route involved getting past German army lines. Nevertheless some POWs did get through to the Allies, one pair making it by bus right through German-held towns.

In the centre of the peninsula, near Servigliano, Jim McMahon had noticed that from the moment the Allies landed in Italy the camp guards seemed to get more lax. On occasions the prisoners were allowed out of the compound to play football. Jim had spotted a deep creek on the edge of the footy ground. Its banks could offer good shelter if the moment came to get away. However, in the weeks following the Italian surrender, it seemed as if escape would be easy. One day early in October POWs were told that the guards would open the prison gates and they were free to go. Then confusion set in. For a while, in the early evening, the gates stayed open and then, just as hastily, were shut again, presumably as the result of countermanding orders. However, Jim and several companions slipped out while they still had the chance.

> We thought if we got into that creek, they wouldn't find us again. There were five Australians and one Scotsman with us and when we got out we walked along this blessed creek. We got pretty tired after we walked quite a way and then we camped on the bank.

The next morning we saw this vineyard and there were still some grapes hanging on the vines there so we had a feed of these grapes. Then we came across some women doing their washing. We were in Italian uniforms you see and they might have thought we were Italian soldiers. But when we saw these women we walked up to them and they still went on doing their washing although they saw us. But as soon as I said, 'I am an Australian,' they were off for their lives and back to their village. Left their washing, ran like hell back to the camp. When we got to their village there was nobody in it. They had disappeared. We changed our clothes, we scrounged around until we got a bit of tucker and we had a feed. We left our uniforms there and we got some old clothes that they had there, and we put them on so that we could walk around in civilian clothes.

For safety reasons the group decided to split up. With Tom Kelly, from the Scots Regiment, Jim decided to head for the mountains in central Italy. There they met and joined a band of partisans now fighting against the fascists and the occupying Germans. They were not the only ones. The mountains were full of escaped prisoners who had thrown in their lot with the Italian left. Cooperation with British intelligence was just beginning and English-speaking partisans like Jim would prove useful recruits.

The partisan network operated right through the mountain spine with links to the plains west and east of the Apennine chain. The band that Jim had joined operated in Ascoli Piceno, in central Italy between Rome and the Adriatic coast. Italian partisan groups represented many different political interests, sometimes with conflicting aims. Nonetheless they all worked in one way or another with the Allied forces. Jim's commander was a Czech who communicated with the five hundred men in his area by field telephone. He was also in radio communication with the RAF.

We'd get instructions. They wanted a bridge blown up somewhere. They'd drop us the dynamite and the fuses and the caps and everything to go with it and then the plungers, an instantaneous fuse, as much as we wanted. They'd say, 'Well we want this certain bridge blown up because we don't want to go over and bomb the place our-selves – if we do we might drop one bomb in the wrong place and since you are there you can blow it up.

Thanks to his mining experience in the Murchison goldfields, Jim soon found himself promoted to chief detonator.

When we went out on a big job I used to have to carry the hand grenades and the dynamite to make up our bombs, to throw at trucks or any enemy vehicles as they passed along the road. They said, you're the only one that's supposed to know anything about explosives. I said, 'Yes, that's right, nobody else will take the job on that's why.' When we went down to blow one of the bridges up none of the others would do it. I said, 'Oh well, I'll do it, as long as you watch on each end of the bridge and make sure and tell me when the convoys are coming so that I can get all the charges ready.' Then we put the instanta-neous fuse in and ran about a couple hundred yards away hooked it onto the plunger and waited until the convoy came. And then when they got about halfway across the bridge we'd just push the plunger and then run like hell back to the mountains because they'd be after us for sure. They had bigger machine-guns than we had and we'd have to run like hell to get back. We'd walk about up to forty kilometres every night and then sleep during the day and then out again the next night somewhere.

Playing the role of a partisan was as risky for a POW as for an

Italian. If caught, saboteurs in civilian clothes were liable to instant execution. There would be no time to plead that you were really an escaped soldier. To add to the risk, the work sometimes meant raids on towns where the fascists still held influence.

> *But we wouldn't go all together. We'd make arrangements to all land there at the same time on a certain hour. Then we'd reconnoitre the place to make sure we had an escape route, if the Germans or the fascists came. (They were worse than the Germans, the fascists.) Then we'd wait until it was dark and go in. The first thing we'd do is go to the police station and find out where all the police were. We'd get them all called back and lock them inside in the police cells. Then we'd go and get the bank managers to open up the banks and get all the lire we wanted out of the banks and then we'd tie up all the big fascist blokes. We'd go up to their places and we'd get all our decent clothes from them, their real suits and that. Well, we had to look smart you know. We'd get around. After that we'd go and open up the grain stores.*
>
> *The church bells would start ringing and the whole population knew what was happening. We'd be at this grain store and they'd have the blooming lot shifted in no time with buckets and bags and bullock carts and every sort of different thing they could get hold of. They'd get rid of all this grain. In three hours it would be all gone.*

Working with the partisans, Jim quickly picked up quite fluent Italian. After one of these raids, flush with cash, he returned to the village where he'd frightened the local women the day after his escape. He had a debt to pay.

> *I gave them some of this money you see, told them that I was one of the ones that had taken their clothes and their food. They said, 'No Australiano, take them, you*

not Australiano, you Italian.' I said, 'No, I'm an Australian.' They said, 'No, you're not!' I said, 'I am.' Then they told me that why they were frightened of Australians was that Mussolini had taught them in the schools that Australians would kill their women and eat their children. That's why they were so frightened of us. Only Australians do that, not the English. If we'd said we were English that would have been all right. But Australians, no. Mussolini had told them to look upon us as convicts you see and Aborigines. They reckoned we were all Aborigines, the ones that 'ate human flesh' you see.

At Ronseca, Dan Black and fellow POWs heard the news of the Italian Armistice on 8 September but the compound gate was still firmly shut two days later. The Italian guards, it seemed, had orders to hold their prisoners. The POWs took the camp gate off its hinges and left. However, Dan and his three comrades didn't attempt an immediate getaway.

We were all free but we still had to live, so most of us went back working for the farmers that we had been working with before. But now the farmers were paying us wages because we were in the middle of the harvest. That went on for about, I suppose about three or four weeks. We felt fairly safe because these farms were isolated, well off the beaten track. But then we heard that the Germans were going round picking up all the POWs from the farms, so the farmers' advice was to get out.

I don't know whether that was because they were worried about our welfare or because the harvest was just over but that's beside the point. Italian people are very good people. I've got nothing but admiration for them. They fed us, they clothed us, and from then we were on our own. We wandered from house to house, making

134

towards what we thought was Switzerland – well the
high mountains for a start.

Jack Dodd set off for freedom too, travelling with fellow POW, George Bray. So did Doug Le-Fevre, accompanied by Norm Terrell. All four hoped to get out of Italy as fast and as safely as possible. Reflecting on their decision nearly fifty years later, they both felt that they should have moved earlier during the chaos that followed Italian withdrawal from the war. In those first days the fascists, with German support, hadn't fully reorganised.

To begin with they didn't go far from Vercelli but entrusted themselves to the country people, lying low, moving carefully from village to village, dressing and trying to look as much like rural Italians as possible, a harder task for tall, fair-haired Jack Dodd than for shorter, Gallic-looking Doug Le-Fevre, whose family came originally from the Channel Islands. Doug knew he was doing fairly well the day he and Norm encountered an official cycling along a country road towards them. The man stopped and asked them to hold his bicycle while he stuck a poster to a tree. This handbill depicted a desperate looking villain and offered several thousand lire for the capture of any escaped Australian prisoner. As he pinned it up, the two Australians chatted with him about the weather and the harvest. The three then shared their lunch in the shade beneath the 'Wanted' notice.

Before long, however, a series of more worrying incidents persuaded Doug Le-Fevre they should make a run for the nearest safe border in neutral Switzerland. They were becoming too much of a risk for the peasant families who sheltered them.

> *What really browned us off and frightened us was that*
> *they took it out on the civilians. The reason we decided*
> *to go to Switzerland was that there were four of us in one*
> *village and we were woken up one morning and told the*
> *Germans were coming. We went off to the nearby* bosci,
> *the nearby wood, and what had happened was that a*

Jack Dodd (second left) and Doug Le-Fevre (right) dressed as Italian youths, October 1943.

squad of Germans had gone to the wrong village and
there were four other unfortunate Australians there,
whom they captured. But they burnt the village down
and they took the menfolk away. Well, we thought this
wasn't good enough. It was bad enough us getting it in
the neck, but for civilians all they were doing was being
good to people. And if you knew the poverty of those
people! So this was why it really struck home!

Phil Loffman took another route but had a similar experience.

We'd been sheltering on this farm for a few weeks and
thought we were pretty good, and then all of a sudden
people from the next village came over there all dithery
and said, 'The Blackshirt fascistis are in the next farm.
They've captured and shot a lot of your blokes.' Three
Australians were made to dig their own graves before
they were shot. One of them reputedly gave a bit of lip
back and had his tongue cut out and then was still put
into his grave.

It was time to move on, time to try to get out of Italy.

Doug Le-Fevre and Jack Dodd were to meet again in Vercelli. They had both contacted Italian partisans and received escape instructions. Neither knew then that the man organising their getaway was John Peck, their ex-fellow POW from Udine. Jack Dodd had only a vague idea of who was masterminding the operation.

There was a guy who was doing a bit of organising. And
I haven't heard of the man since. And it came to my
mind the other day. We talk about Peck's fishpaste. And
I often wonder about that. This guy's name was Johnny
Peck. I never knew him, never knew him at all, only
knew him when he came into the train that was going up

to Switzerland, just saw him briefly. I don't really know who he was.

They are still uncertain whether John Peck went all the way with them on the train. Someone was supposed to accompany them from Vercelli to the border. It was his job to show them where to alight. Jack Dodd reckons he fell asleep on the journey.

This may have happened more than once. John Peck himself recalls one journey when he did fall asleep, from sheer fatigue, while escorting POWs to safety. An hour or so later he awoke in a cold sweat to find the carriage empty and his nineteen escapees gone.

> *I woke with a start, I thought, my God, we've gone past the station, but we hadn't. So it was time to collect them together and to warn them to get off at the stop. I went through the train and there wasn't a prisoner on it! Not one prisoner was on the train, so I assumed they'd all been captured and I'd been so tired that I just hadn't heard all these things happening. But there wasn't one on the train and they'd disappeared.*
>
> *So I got off at the next station intending then to go back. Perhaps they'd got off at the station previously and perhaps there'd be nineteen prisoners wandering around in the country.*
>
> *When I got off this train at a little place called Morotso, I found there were no more trains back that night. I found the German guard who said 'No there are no more trains until six o'clock in the morning, so you'd better go home.' I said, 'Well I don't live here. I made a mistake about the train and I've got to go back.' He said, 'Well, you can't stop on the station or you go into gaol.' I said, 'Well, what can I do?' He said, 'Well, try the hotel,' and then his comrade said, 'But he can't. We occupy the hotel now.'*

*And because it was curfew I wasn't allowed out of
the station and I couldn't stay in the station, and it was
the commonsense of this man's comrade who said 'Well,
if you promise to behave, I'm going off duty now and I
sleep at the hotel. I'll take you over to the hotel and you
can stop with us for the night, and in the early morning
off you go,' and this I did. So I slept that night alongside
the German troops in the hotel.*

The next morning John Peck ate breakfast with his unsuspecting German hosts and left. He hoped he might find news of his lost charges at the next town up the line. On the station he met a woman he knew, a partisan who greeted him with relief. All his prisoners had safely left the train at the prearranged spot but the partisans had worried about his failure to appear with them.

There was an unkind sequel. Members of another partisan band in the village had noticed his enforced stay as the guest of the German army. Peck was now under suspicion as a collaborator. Some months later charges were levelled at him. It took Peck many more months to clear his name as a trustworthy guide.

Peck was an anonymous guide for more train journeys than he could remember, while Jack Dodd and Doug Le-Fevre and their two companions had only one trip to make. However, it was fraught right from the start.

Once they'd made contact with the escape network the pair waited for further instructions. These came swiftly. They were to catch the tram from Taranzo into Vercelli and watch out for a man with a black hat. If he got off they were to follow him. He alighted after several stops and led them towards an old church.

Inside was a treasure trove of disguise, old clothes galore — shabby, inconspicuous coats, shoes, shirts and trousers — which, once on their backs, helped them melt into the Vercelli population. They were then to go to the main station and catch a train to Lake Maggiore, near enough to the Swiss border for them to jump and run when the time came. Nineteen men were to make this trip, including the four Australians.

Doug Le-Fevre went to get the tickets. With his small stature and Gallic appearance, he seemed the best bet.

The train we were supposed to catch was held up through bombing. They then announced on the tannoy that it was due in fifteen minutes. Vercelli has big steps leading up to the station and I was standing there and this German officer came up. And he very nearly caught me out. The quickest way to catch anybody out is to speak to them in their own language. He walked up to me and I made two mistakes. The first one – I should have run away as an Italian would have. But he was about the same size as me so I wasn't worried.

He said in English 'I would say you are English.' And I started to say 'No!' and changed it to 'Non capito!' which is Italian for 'I don't understand'. He said again, 'You are English!' I said, 'Capese nang!' which are the only two words of dialect I know. And they also mean 'I don't understand.' And instead of scooting off like an Italian I stayed put. Of course I'm still there when he came back which was a silly thing to do. He walked all round me and then walked off saying, 'I still think you're English.'

We then went into the waiting room and I pre-tended to read a newspaper to cover my face in case he came back. We sat there and all of a sudden there was a big loud cry. 'The Germans are coming!' The stationmaster was running up and down the platform and everybody was standing to attention. And in comes this gaggle of high brass German officers, walking up and down the platform. Of course we're worried thinking it was us they were looking for. And at last the train pulled in and it was full of young soldiers. They'd be sixteen or seventeen with beautiful pink faces. And you think our army's

Doug Le-Fevre's after escaping from a prisoner of war camp in Italy.

Doug Le-Fevre's 'escape' ticket from Vercelli to Novara. I went to the
station and got four railway tickets. I must check and see if they're
returns. If so, I'll go back and use them.

ragtag, you should have seen that lot. They were machine-gunners and the poor old officers were trying to get them in some sort of order, and the train had difficulty in stopping outside the little red carpet they had laid out. And of course this high brass got out of the train and everybody started saluting and what not.

Of course we thought they'd come for us, having a guilty conscience. But this was the train we had to travel on. And as we walked up to the second-class carriages, with all these young German soldiers pushing past, one of them hit me with his rifle butt. They just thought we were ordinary civilians and, like so many sixteen, seventeen-year-olds, they were asserting their authority, they'd give you a bump on the ribs with something or other.

The rest of the train journey was less eventful. There was one more delay of almost an hour and a half just outside the station. The RAF were paying a visit to Marshal Kesselring's Vercelli headquarters. The train was full of German troops. Jack Dodd was highly conscious of their presence and feigned sleep as much as possible. They had all been told not to utter a word in case they revealed their identity through their accents.

For John Peck, as a guide, every one of these journeys was tense.

When you take these people in heavily populated places, by car or by train, the greatest stress is that every minute, all the time, you have the chance, for whatever silly reason, that something goes wrong, somebody stopping you, somebody asking you a question, somebody being suspicious of your accent or your appearance. And when you've got prisoners on a train, for example, where you can't get off, you're stuck there, with the train going at sixty miles an hour, and there's no hope of getting off except by jumping and almost certainly killing yourself.

Jack Dodd, Doug Le-Fevre and their companions had been told to jump off the train, but only at the right speed and at the right time and place. Once they entered the mountains they were to look out for a big trestle bridge where the train would give a whistle and start to slow. That was where they were to get off. However, Italian and Australian notions of train speed were, and still are, quite different. They heard the whistle, took up positions on the running board as instructed, watched the telephone poles race past like fence posts and only dared to jump as the train began to pick up speed again. They sank into twelve feet of snow and crawled out unhurt.

As arranged, the partisans were waiting to show them their route to freedom over the mountains. They walked all night, sleeping briefly at one stage beneath a pile of dead leaves in the intense cold. Next morning there was one tense moment. They were told to run quickly across a main highway and take cover on the other side. Germans frequently patrolled this route linking Italy and Switzerland. They were lucky. The road was empty. There was one more climb and then another and another. It was a cold, but almost uneventful, end to their escape. Even so, Jack Dodd thought that, almost at the last moment, something had gone badly wrong.

> When we got to the top of the mountain, overlooking the border, we saw all these soldiers. We said, 'We've been given away. We've been tricked,' because they had the same colour uniforms as Italian soldiers wore. And we were inclined to go back. And then we thought, 'We're like sitting ducks up here. They can pick us off easy as anything. What we need to do is go down. There aren't many of them and maybe we can overpower them.'
>
> Well, when we got down, they were Italians all right. Italian border guards on the Italian side of the Swiss border. And they had hot tea ready for us when we got down and gave us some dried meat. That's all they

had there. Of course we felt a great relief. And they were
good to us. They knew we were coming and they said,
'Where's the other two?' (Another pair of escapees.) And
before we left we could see the other two coming down.

For Jack and Doug, reaching Switzerland marked the end of their war. They travelled through unoccupied France and embarked for Australia from Marseilles, returning to Australia separately, Doug arrived home a month earlier than Jack. His wife, Eileen, waiting in Cottesloe, had only just dreamed of his return. A vivid detail was her embarrassment that, when he came back, her hair was in rollers. Not that it mattered, he told her, when the dream came true, right down to the hair rollers.

Jack Dodd came home on New Year's Day 1944 and went straight home to his family at Boyup Brook. The ship on which he was travelling was supposed to put in at Fremantle. However, Japanese submarines were lurking in Australian coastal waters. Warned, their vessel took a wide detour south and made for the port of Melbourne.

Jack and Doug both remained in the army but within Australia, serving in holding camps until hostilities ended a year later.

Dan Black was less lucky when he began his journey to freedom. Like Jack and Doug he headed for Switzerland and made his first hide-out in a small village called Zimone in the Alpine foothills.

It was a farming area but they also grew a lot of grapes
for wines. I'm in this vineyard, and I found a little hut,
so I decided to stay there, and eventually there were four
of us. We all got together because we all wandered in
approximately the same place. We had nothing to eat so
we gathered some tomatoes and some stuff that was
growing around, and made a bit of a stew of it. We tried
to eat it but we couldn't because there was no salt.

So I decided to go down to the village. I spoke a

little bit of Italian. I knew what salt was, it's sale, *and* pane *for bread. I went down there and eventually bought some because we had* lire.

That night the locals asked me a few questions, and I said I trusted the Italian partisans because they were on our side, and that same evening this fellow and his two daughters arrived with enough food to feed a platoon of men: bread, salami, cheese, everything you really needed. He said to us, 'From now on, this is my property, you stay here and you don't move from it within reason, a few hundred yards is all right. We know there are spies in the village, and we want to protect you from those, and we'll come up every night and feed you.'

Well, it was a pretty good offer so we stayed. Then one night just before Christmas 1943, he came and said, 'I'm moving you to another place on the other side of the range.' He said, 'We think that you are in danger of being picked up by the Germans. They're very active.'

The locals, as they did so often, were protecting Allied POWs at the risk of their own lives and those of their families. The Germans had warned them that if they caught any more prisoners within a certain distance of Zimone and other villages they would burn down all the buildings. It was a threat that Dan Black later saw put into action. He was happy to stay away.

We went across the range and we were there about a month. People still kept on feeding us. We were doing nothing – that's how good the people were, and one day we heard some shots. So the four of us wandered down the road and I'd seen these Italian people dressed in Italian uniforms coming towards us, and we'd heard of partisans who were starting up in the area, and we thought they were partisans. I am walking towards this Italian soldier, saying, 'Inglese, Inglese.' It's no good saying Australian, they didn't know what Australians were. So I'm saying, 'Inglese, Inglese,' English, and I looked at him.

By this time I'm about five yards away, and I reckoned he was going to shoot, and he said, 'Mani up.' I knew what that was, it's 'Hands up!' So I put my hands up and stood there, and the others did the same, and the next minute a staff car arrives with a German officer. He jumps out of the staff car, and I said, 'Oh Jesus, we're back in the bloody bag!' Anyhow they took us all to a civilian gaol at Abries.

Dan Black spent Christmas 1943 in prison. The food was poor and conditions hard, however, to his delight and surprise, several nuns and a priest arrived with good news under their cassocks, bread and cigarettes and other items of cheer. With their benefactors the prisoners went to Christmas service in the gaol. But festive cheer was short-lived. Two days later the Germans took their captives to Turin. Compared with Abries, conditions were now far worse. There was little to eat, and the POWs were sent out each day to work for the German army. However, work for the military gave Dan Black another chance of escape.

This day it was cold as hell – January in northern Italy and it was freezing, and the Germans had picked up all the men they wanted, and were ready to go. But they decided they wanted one more man, and they came back into the hut where we were trying to get warm round the tiniest fire you've ever seen. We had a pack of cards there so we picked cards to see who would go out, the last one had to go for the Germans and, of course, I lost – I had to go.

So I went and the job was carting coal from an Italian college for the Germans. I was in the cellar and I'd got the barrow full, and I wheeled it through the kitchen. As I was going out I noticed the German sentry with a cigarette in his mouth, looking for a match. So I went out, dumped the load of coal into the truck, and when I came back the German wasn't at his usual post. There was a door but I didn't know where it led. I dropped the barrow and went through the door, and as I did, I heard a big fellow yell out to me, 'Wait for me!' I said, 'I wait for no bastard – I'm off,' and I was in a long passage. I went up it and got into the front of the college.

I looked round the corner and there was no distur-bance, nobody seemed to be worrying that somebody had got away because they hadn't found out I've gone. I sneaked through the front gate, and I'm in the middle of Turin, and I don't look very much like an Italian. I was dressed in all these dirty civilian clothes, – they never gave us any uniforms. And I thought, 'Well what will I do?' I was covered in coal dust so I looked like a workman. So I slouched through the town.

Turin is a big city to navigate. However, Dan knew the direction he wanted to take. He was heading back towards the scene of his capture, Zimone. Despite the risk, he still had friends there. The journey took two days.

The first night I called into a house for something to eat and they set the dogs on me. It was probably a fascist house. I got further out and went into another house and they gave me some bread and cheese. And while I was eating I could hear the churning of the telephone handle. They were ringing the authorities, so I shoved the food in my pocket and ran.

Away I went. I had no trouble getting over streams because they were all frozen, all the canals were frozen. I could walk over them. I got to the Po River, and I could see a railway bridge and at one end there was an army hut and at the other a sentry box. I didn't know whether the hut was occupied.

Dan decided to risk an entry. To his enormous relief the hut was empty.

I curled up in the corner. I woke up frozen stiff. I had matches and lit a fire on top of the board. I went to sleep curled round the fire, woke up and the whole bloody hut was on fire! So I put it out with snow, and I thought this is bloody stupid! I can't have a fire because I've got no place to light it. I could light a fire outside but I had to be inside because the wind was freezing outside. So I crawled under the hut, took off my coat, put the dirt from under the hut where it wasn't frozen and pulled it out, put it in the other end of the building which wasn't burnt, and put the fire on top of that, and had a good sleep for the rest of the night.

Next day Dan reached Zimone. The same couple who had previously helped him again provided shelter. They even offered him their featherbed on his first night back. Soon, however, the husband warned him that he must move on again.

He came to me and he said, 'Daniel, I'll have to send you up.' He pointed towards the mountains, the Alps. 'See that white building?' I could just make it out, it was twenty-five miles away. 'Well, that's where you've got to go, that is partisan headquarters.' And away I went. I had to go through a big town called Biella, one of the big industrial towns. Well, when I finished up I was that tired I sat down on a log and I started crying from sheer exhaustion.

And I thought well, now that I've lost the only

people in the world I know, the people back in Zimone, I'm on my own, and how am I going to get through this town? Before leaving he'd given me a bottle of grappa, a bottle of wine and some food. So I got out the grappa. I had a few snorts of this and after a couple of minutes I didn't care, I would have fought the bloody Germans barehanded.

I walked through the town, the quickest way I could, still dressed in my old rags, past German and fascist troops, head down, slouching along. I got through and kept on going up the mountains. I got into the snowline and then I heard these people coming down and it was too late to hide. I could hear thump, thump, as they were coming down the pass that I was going up. And it was a mob of partisans, led by the man who was to be my future commander. He was a fellow called Loonden, an Italian Jew (we called him Lungo), and he'd been in London – he'd studied in London to be a lawyer, and he spoke perfect English. So he interviewed me for a couple of minutes. They were going down to do a bit of a raid, and he told me to keep going. 'When you get up there, tell them I sent you, and I said to put you up till I get back.' The Partisan HQ when I got there was a big hotel.

I got up to the third storey – they let me sleep in one of the rooms which was full of bags of hay and things like that, and I think I spent almost three days asleep. Then Loonden came back and interviewed me fully to make sure I wasn't a spy. Anyhow, evidently it worked out all right, and I was now a partisan.

Dan Black's direction had changed. He was the only Australian among fifty Italian partisans and rapidly learned their language and their politics. He had committed himself to the Italian Resistance and the idea of escaping had to take a back seat. At least he was still free.

Phil Loffman was less fortunate. He had gone south hoping to break through to the advancing British and American armies. Things went badly wrong. The Germans arrested him and his two companions. They went straight to a military prison. However, his second prison spell in Italy was to end abruptly. The Germans were pulling out of Northern Italy.

> When they got their orders for the Russian front they threw us on the back of a three-tonner, with a lance-corporal and a driver. And they only went a few miles up the road, pulled into the local car factory – the lance-corporal walked into the machine shop, fired a lethal burst of machine-pistol fire through the roof and said, 'The first thirty blokes on the lathes – onto the back of the trucks!' These poor Italians were all in their blue overalls with their lunch boxes and they were all put on the back of the same truck as us, taken straight up the Brenner Pass into Germany – all slave labourers together.

In his POW camp in Southern Italy, Jack Hawkes was also unlucky. Now, when he thinks about the events of September 1943, he feels that they should all have got up and gone the day the Italians capitulated. They were held back by advice from above.

> This New Zealand officer, he was a padre, he just said, 'Well you should stop here,' and we, silly dopes, we took notice and the Germans were there the next morning and they took us first to Gruppignano and then over to Austria. We arrived in Spittal on 14th of September 1943. Spittal-an-der-Drau, that's what it was called. We left on the 1st of November and we went out to a working camp called Pols – Pols by Udenburg and we lobbed in there on 1st of November.

Phil Loffman and Jack Hawkes were to spend most of the next two years in POW labour camps in Czechoslovakia and Austria. Their moment of freedom finally came with the advance of the Russian army from the east in the spring of 1945. Phil ended his war as he had begun it in Northam, Western Australia, driving a horse and cart towards American lines. The German army had run out of fuel.

Jack Hawkes' military career ended near Salzburg in prison camp Stalag 18B which, with the collapse of the Nazi regime, became a temporary holiday camp. Jack and his companions waited until the Americans flew them out to England. There, both he and Phil Loffman lived it up for several weeks before returning to Australia.

Phil Loffman sailed home on the *Stirling Castle*, through the Panama Canal and into the Pacific. He disembarked in Sydney and came back by train.

> *I'd left Perth station going towards the sea and came back to Perth station from the Nullarbor. So I'd been right round the world at a dollar a day.*

Meanwhile, in Italy, Dan Black, Jim McMahon and John Peck were to remain involved in the battle for the peninsula almost until war's end. In 1943 that looked a long way off.

The struggle for Italy was intense. Despite official repudiation of Mussolini and his regime, and the Italian surrender in September 1943, the fascists were far from finished. Mussolini had held power and commanded their loyalty since 1922. For John Peck they were still very much part of the scene.

> *Every town, every city, every village, had its organised fascist regime, and when the armistice was declared, this was all very well in the part occupied or soon to be occupied by the Allies, but in the rest of the country, it took time for the anti-fascists to come out from under and*

Escaped Australian POWs with Italian guide.

*take over. And in civil administrations there's always a
certain inertia which means you're not able to replace
one regime with another, and besides, there were half-a-
dozen or more political parties which hadn't been allowed
to function for decades and they were in no position to
take over as a going administration.*

*So a lot of the fascists were left in power, albeit to
be a power eventually controlled by the Allies; but above
all, Italy was in the throes of a war on its territory, on its
soil.*

This was a war fought largely by the Germans, contemptuous of
the surrender of their former ally and determined to halt the slow
but inexorable Allied advance up the peninsula. Their army still
held much of northern Italy including key cities such as Milan and
Turin. German troops quickly re-occupied former Italian prisoner-
of-war camps and recaptured Allied prisoners. These POWs were
caught in the middle. The departing Italians had encouraged them
to leave and fend for themselves while the Allies instructed them
to stay in their camps and await liberation. Unfortunately liberation was a long way off. German troops were everywhere and
whenever they found them, swiftly deported escaped POWs north
into Germany and Austria.

Peck's knowledge of the Italian language and landscape were
now to pay off. He arranged staging points, guides and safe houses
along secret routes. Before long he had support and funds from an
anti-fascist committee in Vercelli. Changing his appearance, he
dressed in smart suits and put on a pair of glasses with plain
lenses. To the casual observer, Peck was now a successful Milanese
businessman.

By November 1943 his network had spread from Vercelli to
Turin and Milan and even as far as Genoa on the west coast. He
had also established links with the main organising committee of
the Italian Resistance in Milan. Some of his Italian confederates
from that time were nervous about working with him. He didn't

seem to care about the incredible risks he ran. However, Peck's own description of his work doesn't bear out this impression.

> The risks were enormous. I was always in fear, because even if I did everything correctly, I could have been picked up just casually like anybody else. But with prisoners who were normally much taller than local people, local men, they normally had fair hair, they spoke only English, and they had no knowledge of how and where they were going; they were sheep, led to the slaughter, and in many cases this happened with inexperienced couriers, inexperienced guides.

Peck himself had been betrayed more than once during his resistance work, once while using a genuine identity card, genuine because it belonged to an Italian taken prisoner by the British before Italy surrendered and now safely in captivity in Canada. Peck had gone to the *municippio*, the local town hall, applied for and received a proper identity card complete with photograph and fingerprints.

> Later, when a lot of the organisation members were arrested, somebody betrayed me, and the way they betrayed me was to say who I was and that I was going under the name of this Italian. Our people were given his name to use if necessary. So I used it to get the identity card. And the Blackshirts were told that I was going under the name of so-and-so and I could be found at such-and-such a place.
>
> Well, as it happened I was then taking another group of prisoners to Switzerland, and so when they arrested all the others they missed me. But when I got back from Luino, at the railway station, there were great posters with my picture 'Wanted dead or alive!'
>
> I couldn't work out how they'd got my photograph.

John Peck's photograph which was used on his 'wanted' poster.

But, of course, they'd had further information that I was
travelling under this name. So they went to the town
hall, went through the identification records and there
were my fingerprints and photograph, so they blew it up
and plastered it round.

From now on it was difficult for Peck to remain in his old
haunts. He had become known not only by reputation, but also by
appearance (even if a disguised one) to both the Italian fascists and
the Germans. After an unsuccessful attempt to get fellow resistance workers out of prison in Vercelli, Peck went back to the
organisation's Luino base. Luino lies north of Milan between Lake
Maggiore and Lake Como and almost on the Italian-Swiss border.
Here the Resistance movement was thriving and he was able to
extend its activities, disrupting, German lines of communication
and conducting lightning raids on Blackshirt centres.

Jim McMahon was doing different work but with the same end in
mind, operating from central Italy. In January 1944 his partisan
band had been diverted to Salerno to assist the Anzio landings by
Americans and British troops.

We got the message from the Allies that the Germans
were building up a lot of artillery and tanks and trucks
and everything at Salerno right through to Porto San
Giorgio. They were going to try and hold the line there
when the Allies asked us if we'd go in and see if we
could blow up some of these vehicles, as many as we
could. So about thirty or forty of us went in about two
o'clock in the morning. The Italians in our mob they
reckoned they'd deal with the guards in a very quiet way,
get rid of them.
Then I would go in afterwards and I'd have blokes
with me that would help me put explosives on the tanks
and trucks and armoured cars and hook them up to a

157

John Peck's hideout in Vercelli cathedral (arrowed). Late 1944
– early 1945.

plunger. *We hooked up as many as we could. Then phutt! and off like hell back to the mountains again. It wasn't very far from Salerno back to the mountains. But the Germans never came up the mountains after us and they never bombed us because they had no planes there.*

There was an interesting sequel to the Salerno raid.

When we got back to the camp one of our blokes was missing. About two o'clock the following afternoon this Italian chap, he had been an officer in the Italian army, said, 'Oh well, we'll go back and see if we can find this fellow,' back in Salerno. So the Scotsman (Tom Kelly) who'd been with me all along, this Italian and I, we went down to the nearest village and borrowed some donkeys. We thought riding into town on the donkeys they'd think we were only peasants.

We were riding across this open field and I looked up to the main road and saw Germans. The Italian officer was about fifty yards in front of me and I shouted out to him. Next thing there was a burst of machine-gun fire and the Scotsman's donkey was shot clean from underneath him. I jumped off the one I was on, the Italian jumped off his and started running down to where there was a big creek not far away from us, but I had to run about a hundred yards to get to this creek. Kelly had about seventy or eighty yards to run. I said to him, 'I'll stay here behind this big stone and I'll try and hold them off while you get away,' because I had this little machine-gun with me you see. It was only a Sten gun but still it might help. He said, 'No, come on keep on running.' So I kept on running and running. There were bullets going between my legs and throwing dust all over me. Not one of those bullets hit me. I got back to the bottom of the mountains and we camped in this village

and I was that exhausted that I couldn't have run
another yard when I got there. Then these Italian women
looked after us and made us chicken soup and said, 'All
right, now you can camp up in the loft up there.'
    They knew they might have got into trouble, shelter-
ing us. But I never knew of any that. You see we had a
lot of people around Italy working with us and our scouts.
We had them scattered all over the place. Every time we
went out they would tell us where the Germans were and
what time we would be coming to town and normally
there would be no enemy there.

However, that evening they were. Around midnight that night
the trio heard machine-gun fire. They jumped out of their loft and
raced back up the mountains. There was no time to thank the
women who had sheltered them. However, the Salerno operation
had made them popular with the locals.

    They were thrilled to bits that we were doing this. As a
    matter of fact I had a girlfriend in Italy at the time. She
    lived in Salerno. I've got a photograph of her in my
    wallet. I was pretty well much in love with her for a
    start. When I left her she wasn't too sure about it, she
    didn't want me to go, she wanted to come with me and
    she didn't want to come with me, because she wanted to
    stay and look after her family. She was a dressmaker.
    Every time the Allies dropped something to us whether it
    was dynamite or machine-guns or bullets, it was always
    in a different coloured parachute.
        All these parachutes were made of silk and you
    might get four or five every night. Of course they weren't
    sent back, we'd take them down to the villagers and give
    them the silk. I used to give them to this girlfriend
    because she was a dressmaker. She was really pleased
    with them too. It was good stuff, pure silk. All the vil-

lagers were wearing these silk dresses, and they looked
quite nice in them too.

In the north, Dan Black had not regretted his decision to join the
Italian Resistance.

Because they were armed and they had some chance of
protecting themselves, and also I was under the impres-
sion at that time that British and American troops
fighting around Rome at that time, within a few weeks,
or a couple of months, would arrive up north. So I
thought, 'Well, I'll hang on here with the partisans.' In
the meantime I'm keeping myself occupied. I didn't want
to go back on to that loneliness I felt when I was trying
to get through to Biella and I'd left the only people in the
whole of Europe that I knew, the people in Zimone.

After taking part in a couple of actions with partisan bands,
they considered him fully fledged. He'd picked up enough Italian
to communicate effectively, was given command of a squad called
the *Arditi* (The Keen) and was told to go down to the plains and
create just as much trouble as possible.

They gave me ten men and I was the one that was
always on my toes. I wanted to go down from the moun-
tains. A lot of them were quite prepared to stay in the
mountains and just stay away from the Germans and the
fascists. But I had this silly idea, being young, that I had
to do something while I was there to help the country –
to help the war effort or something like that.
 We attacked a couple of German posts and it was
always a sort of hit and run, but the whole idea of it was
to tie up German troops trying to control the partisans,
keeping them up north so that they couldn't fight the
Allies down south. In addition to doing my little bit for

King and country, I was also helping myself because the more troops we could tie up in the north, the quicker our troops would advance up from the bottom.

However, the Allied troops were not to reach northern Italy until almost the end of the war. Fierce German resistance near the monastery-fortress of Monte Cassino blocked their route to Rome. The Allies were reluctant to destroy this ancient building and its treasures, believing, wrongly as it turned out, that the Germans were inside. German troops certainly occupied the town of Cassino but not the heights above.

Field Marshal Kesselring had already made a secret agreement with the Papacy in Rome whereby the monastery's priceless documents were held safely in the Vatican. The German army benefited for a long time from Allied reluctance to destroy this two-thousand-year-old building. The expected rapid Allied advance slowed down. Moreover, the Germans, with strong transport links back into their own heartland, were still masters of northern Italy. The only resistance they encountered in the north was from partisan units like Dan Black's *Arditi* squad.

We'd get information that there was a German convoy maybe travelling from Milan to Turin, and we'd set up an ambush – and fire on as many trucks as we could and then get away because there were only ten of us and we could only hit and run. We used to blow down the high-tension powerlines and we were getting dropped arms and ammunition. The English were flying over at night and dropping us arms and plastic explosive to blow up rail lines and things like that.

We used to have to listen to Radio London and they would give us the correct signal. For example, if they said, 'The coal is black,' it was a negative, they weren't coming over that night. If they said, 'The snow is white,' that could be a positive.

You had certain call signs for each area, and when
we got that call sign we had to go out at a certain time at
night, and light a triangle of fire with the longest point of
the triangle pointing the way the wind was blowing, so they
would know where to drop it. We used to lose a hell of a
lot of stuff, unless it was a really good drop because it's
hard to drop things accurately in the dark. So sometimes
we finished up with detonators but no plastic explosives.

In March 1944 the Germans sent a very large body of troops
from the plains to try to flush out all the partisans. Dan Black's
men retreated further into the mountains and camped out in a
remote farmhouse.

In the mountains it was very cold, so to keep the place
warm they put the cattle underneath the building and
we'd sleep above them, and the warmth of the cattle kept
us warm. We were all asleep there but we had guards
out, and about daylight the Germans opened up on us
from about a mile away with heavy machine-guns. They
were on an opposite ridge. So we jumped up. Everybody
was running to get out of the hut because the bullets were
coming through the galvanised iron roof and you could
see the holes appearing in one side, and the other side as
they passed through. Well, I pulled on my boots and I got
my submachine gun and my Sam Browne with my pistol
in it, and I reached over to pick it up when a bullet hit
me, but I couldn't see where.

It made a noise something like a sledge-hammer.
Luckily I was leaning over when it hit me. It must have
just missed my head and gone straight through the shed
and out the other side. But now I could see the blood
coming out. I was on my own now, the last to leave.

When I got out on the opposite side to the firing, the
only way I could get down – all the Italians had gone –

*was to throw myself over the side. I landed in the snow
and I had to chase after the Italians. They were all
running up the mountain to get on to the other face. So I
yelled out to my commander, 'Lungo, Lungo!' He said,
'Are you all right?' I said, 'Yes.' He said, 'Can you walk?'
I said, 'Yes.' We got over the other side of the hill out of
the range of the heavy machine-gun.*

*So we got over the other side and when I started to
go downhill I couldn't walk. I could walk uphill but not
downhill – funny thing. So Loonden said, 'Well, we'll
have to get somebody to carry you.' I said, 'You can't
carry me, Lungo, you'll have to leave me.' He said, 'We
can't leave you,' and I said, 'Well, I don't think they'll
come up this far. How about putting me alongside that
heap of rocks there, and covering me up with rocks, a big
rock and smaller ones standing up?' He said, 'Righto.'
And that's what they did and they left me.*

The German soldiers came up the slope towards the improvised
cairn. Daniel could hear their guttural voices, very close to him
now. It was impossible for him to move. His leg had gone numb,
but the intense cold had at least slowed the bleeding. The
Germans continued their search, shouting to each other, but eventually their voices faded away downhill. Two hours went by. Then
he heard a call 'Danielli! Danielli!' The partisans were back. When
they rolled the stones back and extricated Dan, his leg had gone
rigid. He couldn't move it at all.

*The Germans had burnt the farmhouse down, where I
was shot. But they got the door off, put me on it. I'm not
a very small person, and they carried me – must have
carried me five or six miles. Poor buggers! I went over the
route later on and thought how in God's name had those
blokes done it. Of course they were mountaineers, most of
them. They got me to what they called a safe place, and*

*left me there with one bloke. He had drugs there and he
looked after me.*

Given their isolation, there was no way that Dan could get to
see a doctor or go into hospital. However, he was walking again
within six days. Later, in London, during a medical checkup, he
showed the injury to an army doctor. 'You were very, very lucky,'
the doctor told him. The bullet had passed between the bone and
the main artery. If it had hit the main artery, he would have bled
to death, and if it had hit the bone he could easily have died from
gangrene poisoning. Dan could only conclude that he must have
been preserved for something.

At his Luino base in Italy, John Peck and the partisans took
sabotage very seriously. They'd received instructions from the
British authorities in Switzerland to blow up a railway line. The
Germans used this particular route to send coinage through
Switzerland, but not for banking. Minerals were now in short
supply and they were desperate to melt down any quantities of
copper, brass, aluminium and silver coins.

The British had already lodged a protest with the Swiss government, based on international laws on currency and coinage. The
Swiss promptly forbade the Germans to use Switzerland as a
supply route any longer.

Unfazed, the German administration in Italy simply turned old
money into base metal, by the artifice of mechanically defacing
every coin. Soon shipments of high quality metal were again travelling through the Swiss mountain passes and tunnels into
Germany for war matériel. Peck and his team were told to stop this
traffic, literally, in its tracks.

They failed. At the first attempt their explosives didn't go off,
and at the second try John Peck's career as saboteur nearly came to
an unpleasant end. The Gestapo came for him in the middle of
the night.

I was captured in a German officer's uniform. This is one of the things I was wearing to blow up the railway line. We were going to do it in the middle of the night but the Gestapo got there first and so I was already dressed, asleep on the bed, waiting for the time to come.

One of the people involved had unintentionally betrayed us. He'd been at the opera and was overheard boasting to a friend about our exploits, not knowing that in the seat behind him was an informer. The informer sneaked out during the performance, told the Gestapo and the Gestapo came at three o'clock in the morning, arrested him and interrogated him strongly. This had no effect and then they brought his parents and said if he didn't tell them everything they would torture his parents in front of him, and so he gave in and told them all about the organisation.

So that next night I was arrested together with one of the leaders of the organisation, and within forty-eight hours practically every one of the organisation was arrested, and eventually thirty-odd people died, either executed or died in various concentration camps, Dachau and Belsen and places like that. But I wasn't. I was sent to Como and tried because I'd been wearing a German army uniform.

John Peck was tried at Como and sentenced to death by a military tribunal in Turin. He was to await execution in a Gestapo prison at San Vittore, Milan, in February 1944. Within the next few weeks a fellow leader joined him in gaol. Giuseppe Baccigaluppi, or Nino as he was known to John, was a formidable Italian Resistance organiser. He also ran escape networks between Italy and Switzerland. The Gestapo had caught him as well.

He had blamed me for everything and I had blamed him for everything. This was an arrangement we had. In fact,

166

most underground people in Europe had this arrangement
that you would have twenty-four hours to make yourself
scarce if somebody in your organisation was arrested.
After that they were entitled to put all the blame on you.

So, knowing he was safely in Switzerland, I put all
the blame on him. As he knew that I would know very
quickly that he had been arrested, he put all the blame
on me, and we met in this prison. But the Germans
never put two and two together. They never connected us
and so he was then in a position to help me because my
time was getting short.

He managed to get me a pair of socks because when
I was arrested by the Gestapo, they stripped me. They
wouldn't let me wear a German officer's uniform during
the trial and all I had was a very old filthy pair of
trousers, a pair of shoes, no socks, and a shirt. And he
gave me about sixty lire which was all the money he
could find because it was about my last chance to
attempt an escape before execution time.

Baccigaluppi also orchestrated Peck's last chance of survival. He
was awaiting execution, possibly only days away. But, from within
the prison, Baccigaluppi used his influence and his internal
networks. As a result of his efforts, Peck was detailed to work on
the bomb disposal squad. Bomb duty was a cynically motivated
Russian roulette the Gestapo awarded to condemned men. The
work was extremely dangerous but it offered Peck some hope.

Since the RAF was now paying frequent and distinctly
unfriendly visits to Milan almost every day, the chance of getting a
shift outside was good. After a particularly heavy raid Peck's squad
was detailed to work at the Lambratte marshalling yards. Others
were there already. Wives and daughters of some of the condemned prisoners had arrived early and bribed the guards with
wine, food and cigarettes. The guards relaxed and, in a convivial
mood, allowed the women to speak to their menfolk.

John Peck (centre) in Switzerland after his escape from San Vittore prison.

It was Peck's best chance to escape. The team, and the German guards, with a break for a particularly good lunch, had worked for about three hours,

when the RAF came over bombing. We were in the holes digging out unexploded bombs which were liable to go off in sympathy with the new bombing explosions. So the guards and prisoners scattered and when I came to the top of the hole, the only one left was the officer in charge who was quite drunk by now (he'd been drinking steadily all day), and I asked permission to run to shelter and he said, 'Yes. There is no one as brave as a German officer. I'm staying here.'

So I said goodbye to him and ran but I ran into the bombing and away from where the guards were. He started shooting but nothing happened – a few bullets went near but that was all. I eventually broke into the bombing area and got away from the execution platoon.

With me was an Italian who was down the hole with me at the time and we decided that we would get into Milan centre itself, but we would not tell each other what we were going to do or where we were going in case we were recaptured and one couldn't give the other one away.

So we jumped over an embankment into the city and, by arrangement, he took the first tram along and I took the second one along, no matter where they were going, and I eventually ended up at the central railway station and got a train to Novara.

Later, I stopped all night in the rice fields and in the early morning got a train from Novara to Intra where I'd been before with the last prisoners. I finally arrived in Switzerland on the 22 May 1944.

For John Peck, the war was still not quite over; however, he had at last broken a continual cycle of captivity and daily risk of death. Many other Australians were still held as prisoners. Others were continuing to fight with the partisans. They also hoped to break that cycle. It was time to go, if they could.

All Allied POWs in enemy territory are to make their way to the nearest neutral territory. This is an order.

That was the message Dan Black and fellow escapee Stan Peeble heard in the autumn of 1944. In their mountain shelter in northern Italy they were listening to Radio London.

Dan Black wondered why they were being told to move. In a way, however, he felt relief. He had noticed a change coming over the partisans.

They were getting very ruthless. They were shooting people every day and I got the feeling that, because I wasn't a communist, I wasn't really safe. I said to Stan Peeble, 'I think they want us out because there is a chance that the partisans, being Communist-led, will use us as a bargaining tool, bargaining for the power to take over the northern part of Italy when the war us over.'

He had seen for himself the savagery that was part of the Italian civil war. In many ways the Communists were as violent in their methods as the Blackshirts they were fighting. Families set themselves against other families often from the same village and he witnessed acts of savagery that sickened him.

I went down with a squad (I wasn't the leader) to the village of Polenya, and I said, 'What have we come down here for?' And they said, 'There's a couple of spies in the village and we're going to pick them up.' I said, 'What are you going to do with them?' 'Oh,' they said, 'we'll take them up the mountains and interrogate them.' I was the only one armed at that time with a submachine gun. We got to the door of this house and they said, 'Righto, Dan, you break in, kick the door in and in you go. You've got the submachine gun.'

We got in there, and there were three fascist soldiers (Republicans they called themselves), two women and a couple of little children. Loonden said to me, 'Right, Danielli, you get these blokes outside while we talk to these women.' The fascist sergeant had a pistol and I took it off him.

So we got outside and I saw this bloke fumbling in his pocket. He was trying to get a hand grenade out. We got that off him. Then we waited. It was about midnight, pitch black. You couldn't see your finger in front of your face. Loonden and Giouo came out and said, 'Come on, Danielli.'

We got on this road which skirts round the village which is cut into the side of the mountain, and there's a hell of a drop on the right-hand side and we were going along. Suddenly one of the Italian soldiers made a break and dropped over the side of the road into the ravine. I swung round and fired a burst after him, but he was well down and we couldn't see a thing so Loonden said, 'Leave him, leave him. I think he's gone. I think you've got him.' Away we go. Loonden said, 'Danielli, you get about fifty yards in front of us in case we run into any trouble. You've got the submachine gun.'

We got in front of the campa santos. That's the graveyard, the camp of saints, and I was about fifty yards in front, and then bing, bang, bing, and I thought, 'Oh hell, we're being attacked from behind! I went straight to ground. I couldn't think what was going on so I got up and I went back, and they'd shot the two women and the two soldiers, they'd shot them dead in front of the grave-yard. I said, 'Loonden, what did you do this for?' 'They

171

were fascists,' he said! 'But why did you shoot the women?' I said, 'The children!' 'They were spies', he said, 'and they entertained these fascists.' The two children were running around, 'No, no, mama, mama,' and the gurgles coming from these poor dead people. I said, 'What are you going to do with the children?' He said, 'Don't worry about that, there will be somebody up here shortly. They'll find the children.' It was the worst shock of my life!

After that incident, Dan felt the squad would not allow him on any more execution raids. His fellow partisans had acquired their ruthlessness fighting against Franco during the Spanish Civil War. Later, they reinforced their experience with guerilla training in the USSR. They had shot the women, they told him, as a warning to others. It was not Dan's notion of fighting a war. But his protest had made his own position dangerous. He had failed to show solidarity over the executions. It was time to part company with the partisans.

I said to Stan, 'We'd better get out!' 'How?' he said, 'It's nearly November, the snow is flying and we've got to get over the mountains into Switzerland. We can't get over this time of the year.'

Snow or no snow, the pair began their exit early in December, taking a third Australian with them, George Mullens, who had been hiding in the mountains since September. The villagers had begged him to take George, as it was becomingly increasingly dangerous to keep him away from the eyes of the Germans. The trio then headed for Monte Rosa, where they learned they would need guides and equipment to get them through the winter conditions into Switzerland.

We'd run out of money and we couldn't get any guides. I

sold my watch to one of the innkeepers there, that kept us going another couple of days. And then one day a fellow came down the mountain with a haversack on his back and said, 'Danielli, what are you doing here?' And it was a fellow called Giorgio. He was a courier and he was bringing cash from Switzerland into northern Italy for the partisans, and the pack he was carrying was full of money. He said, 'What's the matter?' I said, 'Well, we're stranded here. We can't get any money and we can't get any guides to take us over.' He took the pack off and said, 'Here, will that do you?' and he gave us thousands of lire. 'I'll get you to sign for that,' and I signed for it and away he went.

The guides Dan found the next day were smugglers who were on parole. If they were caught inside the Swiss border again they would be unlikely to leave it. However, they agreed to take the three Australians as far as the frontier. They were to meet early one morning.

Dan almost missed the rendezvous. They had all fallen into a deep sleep the night before and woke up several minutes after the agreed departure time and some distance from the starting point. When they arrived at the base of the mountain, Dan saw three figures on skis some five hundred feet above them. He fired his pistol into the air, the sound ringing right round the valley. One man detached himself and sped back towards them. They were on their way at last.

The journey was hazardous in the extreme. At one point, crossing a glacial flow, they had to make their way hand after foot, foot after hand, planting frozen limbs into holes cut just ahead of them by their guides. One slip meant a fall of more than a thousand feet, into the icy lip of a crevasse. Despite the hazards they made it across the mountain barrier, reached the valley floor and the neutrality of Switzerland. Swiss guards picked them up and gave them food and shelter. However, they were still not free.

> They put us through a delousing process, issued us with uniforms, British uniforms, and then sent us to a concentration camp. The camp was full of Poles and Russians, Latvians, all people from the Baltic regions. I said, 'I think there's been a blunder because we shouldn't be in here.' But the Swiss people, they acted like Germans, they wouldn't listen to us.
>
> Anyhow, the following morning we were going through to see a doctor and I was complaining bitterly and arguing with the Swiss official that we shouldn't be there, and in the excitement I dropped a cigarette butt. The Swiss said, 'Pick that butt up!' And you can imagine what I said, and there was nearly a fight as to who was going to get the upper hand. I said, 'No, I'm not going to pick it up because we shouldn't be here.' I didn't mind making a bit of a scene because I thought it was the only way to get some action.

If he couldn't convince officialdom, Dan had more luck with the doctor who spoke perfect English. While he was explaining their predicament, a call came through. The doctor put the phone down. 'There's been a blunder. You and your friends can go back. You shouldn't be here, you should have been sent straight back to France and then on to England.'

The three Australians now learned they would be accompanied to Berne and handed over to the British. Their escort was the Swiss official Dan had nearly come to blows with the previous day.

At Berne the British Consul greeted Dan and his companions. He confirmed that they were now free men. All they had to do was catch a train to Geneva, and from there go through Lyons in France. They were given tickets to travel on their own and were to report to the British headquarters, at Lyons. However, when they reached Lyons the British had moved on and they reported instead to American headquarters.

We went to this beautiful big hotel, reported to an American, told him why we were there, and they gave us a room in the hotel and then forgot about us. Ten days later we were still there and we can't get any sense out of them. 'What are you complaining about? You're getting fed, you've got a room. The war is still going on and it will be over shortly.' I said, 'We want to get back to England.'

Anyhow we couldn't get any sense out of them. So I said, 'Come on, out to the airport. See if we can find a Pom out at the airport. He'll make it right.' Running round the airport we found one lone English major. I went up to him, saluted and told him the position. He said, 'Well what do you expect me to do to help you?' I said, 'Well the Yanks don't care if we stay here to the end of the war. Can't you get us back to England?' He said, 'Why should an Australian want to go to England?' I said, 'Because I was born in the UK.' So he said, 'Look, I've got a plane leaving with mailbags. You'll have to sit on mailbags.' It was an old Dakota, DC3, and we sat on the mailbags and flew about four hours to Paris and then across the Channel. And when we landed at Croydon Airport I kissed the ground and the Pope's been doing it ever since.

Almost immediately he was sent to Eastbourne on the English south coast and later debriefed. Despite the fact that he had fought alongside partisans, British Intelligence were more interested in Dan's knowledge of industrial targets the RAF could usefully bomb in northern Italy than in what he could tell them about the Italian Resistance.

After six weeks the goodwill ran out and Dan and his comrades sailed home. They reached Melbourne in time for the Easter holiday in 1945. On this occasion he did not kiss the soil of Victoria.

In Central Italy, Jim McMahon and his faithful Scots mate, Tom Kelly, were still with the partisans. Unlike Dan, they hadn't received orders to move on. However, they too had begun to think of rejoining their own forces. The Allied advance on both sides of the Apennines made it obvious that the war would end soon for the Germans remaining in Italy.

> One Australian bloke gave himself up to the Germans in Salerno. When they left there they left him behind. I was in a town one day and a German patrol pulled up and there were some Yanks (they were wandering loose in Italy too, they could speak pretty good Italian you see).
>
> But I was in this cafe with Tom Kelly, and this German convoy pulled up and there was a Yank outside, and a German officer walked up to him and said, 'Am I on the right road to Salerno?' And the American said, 'Oh, don't understand Englisee, parlez Italian?' The German officer looked at him and he said, 'Look, I know what you are,' he said, 'You're not an Italian, you're a Yank, you've got Yankee boots on.'
>
> You know what he did, this German officer, he said, 'Have you got a smoke?' And the Yank said, 'No,' He put his hand in his pocket, pulled out a packet of cigarettes and said, 'Here you are you can have them but get the hell off the main roads. We don't want to take you prisoner, we don't know what to do with you.' But if they'd caught us and found we were fighting with the partisans it might have been different.

It was time to go. Both planned to rejoin the 8th Army now advancing up the Adriatic coast. On 30 June 1944 they shook hands with their former comrades and turned south.

> We took all our gear with us, a machine-gun that we had, the Sten guns and a couple of pistols I had, and a

A troop transport ship delivers soldiers who fought in North Africa home to Melbourne.

couple of grenades in case we ran into Jerries, of course. We were going for about ten days and then I said to Tom, 'I think we must be getting pretty near the 8th Army lines.' So we got up and started to walk, straight out towards them. Then we saw this patrol coming and I said, 'They don't look like British troops but they're certainly not Germans.' When they caught up with us they were Polish.

Well, of course, they took us prisoner and they took us back to the 8th Army lines and threw us in a gaol with some Germans and Italians that they had there. More or less told us that they were going to shoot us the next day. Took all our gear off us, the machine-gun, the pistols and hand grenades that we had. But there was a senior Polish officer who could talk a bit of English. I said to him, 'Well, what about getting an English security man to come and see us.' He said, 'All right tomorrow, maybe, if we don't shoot you first.'

They did get a British Intelligence officer. Well, he grilled us for about twenty-four hours. Kelly was all right, he could understand him, he knew he was all right. But me, he thought I was a real Italian, you know. He said 'You look like an Italian, you could be anything.'

Anyway eventually I proved to him that I was certainly an Australian. Kelly had to go back to his own unit which was with the 8th Army, and I never saw him again after that. But a couple of days later when the line started to move up north this officer said to me, 'Well, you can sit in the front of one of the trucks and travel with us.' I was given an English army uniform. Then as we travelled up the coast, we got up past where Tom Kelly and I were in the line to Porto San Giorgio, a place called Ancarano.

Further north we started to pick up a few other Australian stragglers you see. Well, by the time we got right up north, there were fifteen of us Australians all together. And then they said, 'Well, we'll put you on the train and send you back to Naples down the other side of Italy.' So the fifteen of us proceeded down to Naples on this train.

Jim had first seen Italy from the Adriatic side. Now he was to leave from the west coast and retrace his route homeward to Australia by way of Cairo and Bombay. His first taste of home was an old government building in Melbourne.

I've never been so flaming cold in all my life. They wouldn't let us out to go down to the pubs so we used to have to sneak out at night to the pub. They'd come round on a bus every day to take us all round up in the hills. They looked after us like lords for this fortnight. There were only six of us coming back to Western Australia and a few to South Australia as well. The rest were sent on leave straightaway to their home towns in the east you see.

Just six of us just came back to Western Australia. When we got near Kalgoorlie the reporters came out to the train and met us. And then this big column came out in the West Australian the next day. 'R J McMahon and his five companions.' When we got to Perth, they had a Red Cross car waiting for us to take us to where we wanted to go.

John Peck was still moving frequently between Italy and Switzerland throughout 1944. For him the war had not ended. Although he had escaped from San Vittore Gaol and a death sentence, he still felt committed to the partisans.

I contacted our undercover people there and was taken to San Giulio in the northern part of Switzerland where I

179

made my reports and remained for a couple of months for rest and recuperation, and returned to Italy as liaison officer with the Communist partisans, the Garibaldi brigade.

In many ways the war in the north had not gone well for them. They suffered from lack of political unity and the German army's continued strength. But we now had a chance of changing it by partisan attacks in all of northern and central Italy, and in particular in Piedmont where the four different political party partisans really joined together and made coordinated attacks over a large area of the north bordering on Switzerland. We eventually captured an area and called it the Republic of Domodossola. This we kept and fought battles on the periphery until October 1944 when the Germans eventually overran the whole area and what was left of us, the remnants, were forced to retreat into Switzerland.

Peck's own military position had become very complicated by this time. In the Australian army he'd been a private and, as far as the Australian army was concerned, that was the rank he still held. The British army, however, gave him a short-term commission in recognition of his work as a Resistance organiser. He returned to Italy as a temporary captain.

In the strange position of doing what I could for the Allies in that area, part of which was liaison with the partisans, and part of which was to pass on my experience, which was by this time quite extensive over about five years of war, and especially behind-the-lines war.

The Communist formations Peck had fought with were very well-organised and well-led, but many non-Communist resistance groups lacked military experience. To remedy this the unified command in Domodossola asked Peck to leave the Communists and serve with their own division as commander in the central part of the front. The work involved both defence and counterattack. The front they were to defend was a vital corridor. Through it for a hundred and fifty kilometres ran all the roads and railways from the front and through the Simplon Pass into Switzerland.

> This was guerilla warfare except that it was now on a static front which is a very dangerous thing for guerillas, unless backed up by enough organised supplies and reinforcements and equipment, which the partisans weren't.

The British had promised aid to the partisans in northern Italy but when it came it was a trickle, a few dozen airdrops of ammunition and equipment. Priorities had shifted. The Allies were now sending arms into Warsaw to support the Poles in their ill-fated August 1944 uprising. That left Peck and his fellow partisans fighting a much better-equipped enemy.

> It meant that when the Germans attacked you could hold them up for a certain amount of time but they had armour, and in my division, we had one antitank gun, and it was a prewar antitank gun. So the odds were so great that the end was inevitable right from the beginning. I think the total time of holding it was somewhere in the region of forty days, and there are an enormous number of casualties when you're fighting with small arms against armour and heavy machine-guns and artillery.

Eventually the Germans forced the partisan forces out of the valleys and back to Domodossola. Some dispersed and went back into the high mountains again. There they could regroup and fight another day.

Peck's own formation fought its way out but eventually had to retreat up the St James Pass and into neutral Switzerland. There they had to lay down their arms. For John Peck, at last, the war was over.

It was over for many more. Millions had not survived the six years of conflict. The gas chambers of Auschwitz, Dachau and Belsen had almost succeeded in silencing an entire race. Throughout Europe families had been separated, divided by politics war, distance and death. Entire communities had been obliterated and refugees tramped the roads of their own countries, trying to find evidence of the world they had known before 1939. Even for those who had come through, there were many years of displacement to cope with, painful adjustments to a world, which in 1945, was almost unrecognisable.

John Peck (second left) in Domodossola with partisans.

Pasquale Amato and his family as naturalised Australians, 1954.

POSTSCRIPTS

H alf a century has slipped away since the end of World War Two. Today the grandchildren and great grandchildren of those who went through internment or imprisonment are only vaguely aware of that conflict and its origins. But for those who were caught up in the backwash of a war that spread across both hemispheres, the experience is indelible.

For Italo-Australians who either suffered directly from internment or whose families suffered in the process, there was belated but welcome recognition almost fifty years on. Several of the internees who told their stories in Chapter One of this book, and many more besides, were present at a special dinner given in their honour by the Western Australian Government in 1991. State Premier Carmen Lawrence acknowledged, on behalf of former wartime governments, what had obviously been undeserved treatment.

> *It is not my purpose to apologise for the mistakes of the Federal and State governments of the time. The decisions and policies were made in an atmosphere of confusion, suspicion and uncertainty. It's far easier to criticise past mistakes than to work to ensure that those mistakes will not be repeated in the future. The only way to avoid repeating mistakes is to study and to learn from them.*
>
> *In 1939 a large proportion of Australia's Italian*

residents lived in Western Australia, largely because of the rejuvenation of the gold industry and the availability of jobs, and it was in Western Australia that the largest number of Italians was interned. The internments were carried out under the provisions of the National Securities Regulations of 1939, which were, in hindsight, extremely harsh. Those who faced immediate internment included not only those who were suspected of espionage or of belonging to Communist or fascist organisations but also those whose occupations were thought to offer any opportunity whatever for espionage or sabotage.

At the end of the war some internees and their families felt they'd never be able to feel at home in Australia and took the first opportunity to leave. Others, however, and that includes all those here, looked on Australia as their home and their future and they were determined to put the internment behind them and start afresh.

As one internee said, 'The war is over now and we want to forget about it. I want to work and do well. Probably one day we'll buy a home away from here and my children will be considered one hundred per cent Australians. I would be sorry if they had to suffer like some of my kind.'

I want to thank all of you here tonight for the extraordinary courage and determination you showed in staying here and rebuilding your lives. Forty-six years have now passed since the end of the war. On the one hand they seem a very long time to wait for a formal reconciliation. On the other it could be argued that Italians and Australians in the wider community have lived at peace with each other since the war so there's no need for reconciliation. Indeed the most remarkable aspect of the whole internment experience has been the willingness of the internees to put the past behind them and to refuse to be embittered.

Joe, Frank and Con Iannello went back to their peacetime lives after 1945. Frank died in 1994, aged eighty-three. Joe believes he never really recovered either in spirit or in fortune from his long spell of internment.

At the end of the war the Iannello family received eight hundred pounds compensation for the loss of their boat *Dante* in Papua New Guinea. It cost them eight thousand pounds to build the *Dante II*.

Joe resumed his trade as a barber and has only recently retired. Today Joe and Frances Iannello's children work in banking, real estate, industrial chemistry and local government. Joe's brother, Con, took over the family's fishing interest when their father, Colegro died, aged seventy-four. He has also just ceased full-time work.

Dominic Della Vedova and his family resumed their farming life in Pemberton after the war and remained well-liked and respected settlers in the district. Their three children, in turn, gave them eighteen grand-children, who now work in farming, university teaching and in business.

Dominic was forgiving about his time in prison. He told his own children that the war was over, they should forget it and get on with the future.

One evening, some four years after the war, he was asked, along with other members of the Manjimup Rotary Club, to speak about the past. Dominic described his regret at having thought better of Mussolini and the price he had paid for it. The members listened in silence. Another club member expressed the view of the meeting.

Let us never forget the wrong done to Dominic Della Vedova.

Later, in 1956, he and his wife, Elisabetta, paid a return visit to their former home in Italy. They had only been in Baruffini for two weeks when the local *carabinieri* paid a visit. Why, they wanted to know, was Signor Della Vedova, an Australian and a foreigner, in Italy without a visa. Dominic took them to task.

I fought for my country in the First World War. They put me in prison in my new country in the second one. And now, you want to put me in prison when I come back to my old one.

This time he didn't go inside.

In 1945 Maria Panetta married Dominic Baggetta. She had not known him at the time of his internment, two years earlier. The potato-growing scheme he and his father had set up did not work out and Dominic, as he had before the war, travelled anywhere to find work. He was often away for a fortnight at a time, but always returned with money for Maria to keep ahead of the bills. He would kiss his sleeping children, snatch some sleep himself and head back early in the morning to his current job in the bush. Later he found a permanent job with the Public Works Department and their fortunes improved. When the family could afford drives in the country, Dominic would point to a clearing in the timber or a line of fencing and say proudly, 'My hands did that.'

Apart from bringing up her family, Maria Baggetta has spent much of her time working in the Harvey community. She does voluntary work for the elderly and infirm and has served in several community organisations.

Travellers passing through the pleasant rural town of Harvey today may only see one reminder of the internment of many Italian citizens between 1940 and 1942. Just north of the town, as the road winds upwards out of the Harvey river valley, a memorial roadside shrine stands against the backdrop of the Darling Range. The shrine, constructed by the internees in 1940, was intended to be a chapel. It has now been listed as a National Trust site.

Adele Levis' market gardening family had escaped internment and the worst of its consequences. After the war, through continual

189

The Harvey Internment Camp Memorial Shrine.

hard work, they heaved themselves out of the poverty trap that had threatened the early years of their emigration. When the war ended:

> We felt free to live like the rest of the Australians, free from surveillance. It was a good feeling. Until then you felt kept out of the warm circle. You felt excluded. Australia was a baby then. It saw part of its own population as a threat. There was no threat. I could understand then how the Aborigines felt.

Internment had disrupted Italian family life and fortune and many families took a long time to get over it. It also divided the Italian community. Some resented the 'good luck' of those who had not been interned and could never reconcile themselves to their own misfortune.

Men, and some women, had spent time in prison and partners had worked prodigiously to keep a business or a home going. However, at least, for some of that time, wives could visit their spouses and know where they were.

In Italy itself, wives of prisoners of war would not see their husbands until well after the war ended. After the war, as in Australia, families had to rebuild their relationships. Moreover, for families in Italy the conflict had not been some distant event, read about in newspapers or heard over the wireless but far too close for any kind of comfort.

Bruno Anghinetti returned to his village to find that German tanks had run over the family vines and his favourite horse had been commandeered or stolen. The countryside was devastated and there was little to eat.

For his wife-to-be, then Rena Gonizzi, in the village of Riano, near Parma, the war had been just as difficult and almost as dangerous as for her fiancé. Her father and brother were determined to keep neutral in the final struggle for northern Italy between the partisans and the remaining *fascisti*. They had constructed a secret

191

room in the house where they could both hide to avoid forced recruitment into either camp. On one occasion a Blackshirt brigade came to the house and demanded to know where the two men were. They had in fact been warned and fled. However, the sight of male pyjamas convinced the leader that they were not far away.

Fortunately Rena's family had continually kept them at bay with supplies of food. This alone dissuaded the fascists from summary retribution on the family. But there was still a price on her father's and brother's head until the final routing of the fascists in that part of the peninsula.

Bruno returned in 1946, coming from Naples to Milan in an open cattle truck through the devastated landscape of postwar Italy. However, his own family had survived and Rena was still waiting for him. She had heard so many times that he was coming that when he finally arrived, she could hardly believe it. They married and soon had a baby daughter. For a young family, however, in war-wrecked Italy, the times were hard. Australia still beckoned.

The Smiths had always told him that he would be welcome back in Busselton, should he decide to return. However, it wasn't easy. After the first wave of postwar immigration the Commonwealth Government tightened up the rules about desirable applicants. The specific trades and skills they sought did not, apparently, include farm work. Bruno Anghinetti's application languished until a vigorous campaign by a local member of Parliament, Stuart Bovell, on behalf of both the Smiths and the Anghinettis, ensured his acceptance.

Margaret Smith went up to Perth to sign the papers and within twenty-four hours permission came through. Bruno, Rena and their baby daughter were on their way to Australia. They arrived in 1950. The Smith family had helped them with a loan for the fare and offered them employment when Bruno, once again, arrived in the South-West.

Rena Anghinetti had imagined from Bruno's descriptions that

192

all Australians spoke Italian. After all, Bruno had spoken of the Smith family as friends. She was dismayed to find that she was expected to speak English in this strange new country. On the first day she practised saying, 'Good morning Mrs Smith' but forgot the 'Mrs Smith' bit. Just saying 'Good morning!' was hard enough at first. But gradually, as Bruno had had to do in wartime, she acquired English.

Today Bruno Anghinetti has retired and Stephen Smith has handed over more farm work to his own sons. The families are still friends, go to each others' weddings, frequently call and exchange home-grown fruit and vegetables.

On his return to his native land Pasquale Amato found Italy was not the way it was before the war.

> There was a lot of 'black market' and 'corruption' and that was what made me decide to come back to Australia. I had plenty of work but any country which the army has gone through, and not just one army, German, English, American has gone through – then the country changes a lot.

Pasquale and his new wife, Filomena, returned to Australia in 1949. His regular correspondence with his wartime hosts, the Garnetts, had resulted in an offer of sponsorship. Their first child, a daughter, Margherita, was conceived in Italy and born in Australia. For Filomena Amato the long journey from Fremantle to Gnowangerup was much as her husband had seen it five years earlier, 'nothing but bush, bush everywhere'.

Filomena had expected a country much like the America of popular imagination. But the deserted and dark railway stations they passed through, lit fitfully by a single railwayman swinging his lantern, looked nothing like any scene she could imagine. The train wound on again into the unending darkness of the bush. There were no friendly villages, nothing but the vastness Pasquale had come to know and to which he was now determined to return.

Their first job was work on the Garnett farm. Pasquale earned four pounds a week. The Garnetts provided the young couple with a house, furniture, firewood and food. Three more children were born, Maria, Stephen and Angelo. Pasquale later set up in business on his own, first in building, learning bricklaying skills from his brother-in-law, who had also emigrated after the war from the same village of Grassano.

In time, Pasquale Amato became first a contract builder and then ran a restaurant in the Great Southern town of Katanning. He became an unofficial recruiting agent for families from his original village, migrants encouraged by the Amato family success, who also came to settle in Western Australia.

Friendship with the Garnett family survived the postwar years, for both Pasquale and Filomena.

The war had been lonely enough for Luigi Bassano, after his capture. But at least he was out of the fighting. Back in San Vito, his wife, Maria, and her daughters had endured the horror of war in their own land. German troops had driven them from their homes into the countryside. The family home had been bombed and Maria had lost much of her furniture. However, thanks to the strong network of support and cooperation between family, friends and neighbours they coped and survived right through the war without a breadwinner.

From Australia, Prudence Broad had helped too. She had kept in touch with Maria Bassano and her family from the time Luigi first came to their farm in 1943.

> We used to pack up parcels of dress materials. The girls could sew and mother could sew and she used to make all the children's clothing and keep them dressed.

It was well after war's end when Luigi came home to San

194

Anna Bassano wearing a dress made of material sent to her by the Broad family.

Vito. As Maria recalls, throughout 1946, familiar, if older, faces reappeared in small Italian towns. Prisoners were coming home every day. But not, it seemed, Luigi. So when neighbours called out to her, 'Your husband is here,' she couldn't believe it!

It had been eight years since Luigi had seen his family. His daughters Anna and Vita had been six and three when he left for North Africa. They were now teenagers and had grown up as children of a single parent.

His daughter Vita felt that, 'He was a stranger to us and we had to get used to him.'

For Luigi himself, his wartime life in Australia had become the reality he saw for the future. Quite apart from his despair at the destruction of his country by war, he found the climate cold and damp and yearned for the dry, warm spaces of Australia. Prudence Broad and her husband Roy, received frequent letters from him asking him to support his return to Australia, support they were happy to give. By 1949 Luigi had left his wife and children again and was back in Western Australia preparing the ground for the family's arrival. Roy Broad loaned him the two-hundred-pound fare and gave him work on the farm for several months.

For a while Luigi resumed something like his old POW life, feeding the pigs and doing general farm work. He then started work as a bricklayer, working with his son-in-law, Donato Paolucci, a skilled builder whom the Broads had also sponsored. The Broads gave them a US war surplus pyramid tent from which they lived and worked. Donato and Luigi built their first three houses in the nearby country town of York and completely repaid their debt to the Broads.

The rest of the family joined them in 1952. Again, Prudence and Roy Broad helped them with a loan for the fare, money which the Bassanos also repaid within a few years.

Maria had not wanted to come to Australia. She knew no English and was leaving not only her country behind but friends and relations with whom she had shared the hardest of times, and whose company she would miss in the postwar peace. She was delighted to be with Luigi again, but when the family reunited at Fremantle and her husband told her they would soon be at York, the journey seemed to take forever. As they climbed the Darling Range and the lights of Perth faded behind them, Maria found the space and the silence appalling.

Whereas in San Vito she had been surrounded by the sound and sight of human contact, here the bush stretched on forever, silent and alien. When they reached their small house, some five kilometres from York on the western edge of the Wheatbelt, Luigi told his wife there was no electricity; he would have to light up a lantern to show them their new home. She asked him, 'What have we done wrong that you bring us here?'

Anna and Vita felt much the same. They had left teenage friends, their language and their culture behind for the unknown quantity and quality of postwar Australia. By her own admission, Vita:

> ... didn't understand anything, the culture, the heat and the flies!

Nevertheless, they settled and survived. Luigi worked in the York district until he retired. He spent a year with the railways and later became a gardener in the town hospital. He retired to the Perth suburb of Gosnells. His wife, Maria, is now in her eighties and he is survived by four daughters and eight great-grandchildren. Two more Bassano daughters were born after the war, Silvana in 1947 in San Vito, Italy, and Maria Antoinetta in York, Western Australia in 1958. Today their grandchildren work as engineers, housewives, electricians, teachers and medical technologists.

During the 1980s, the Italian government in Rome discovered that Luigi Bassano deserved military commendation for 'an act of bravery' in the campaign in North Africa. Due to his ability to read signals, he had correctly anticipated that a British company was close by and waiting to ambush his own troops. The Italian Consulate in Perth informed him that they wished to present him

Anna (nee Bassano) and Don Paolucci with Prudence and Roy Broad, 1973.

with a medal of recognition at a small ceremony. According to his family, when Luigi received his medal from the Consul, he looked at him and replied that he would rather have had the missing seven years of his life than the decorative piece of brass. The Consul made no comment.

Throughout the Australian part of his life, Luigi continued to think himself lucky, despite the seven-year wartime separation from his family.

> I was first in Ethiopia, then India. Australia was a blessing after that. What would have happened if they hadn't let me come to Australia. What would have become of me?

The Broad and Bassano families are still in touch though time and the passing of older members of each family have weakened the bonds.

Almost from the time Giuseppe (Joe) Varone had first arrived on their farm at Hyden, Doreen Marsh began to make up small parcels of baby powder, soap and little treats for Giuseppe's wife and children back in Italy, a practice she continued after the war ended and Giuseppe had returned to Italy. The Varone family lived in central Italy, not far from the hotly contested town of Cassino. German resistance to the Allied advance had been fierce and determined. The Varones were among the many civilian casualties. They fled from the fighting at its most intense and returned to find their village in ruins. That was also how Giuseppe saw it when he returned.

Back in Australia, Arthur and Doreen Marsh noticed the despair in his letters. He was not finding it easy to take up his old life as a farmer in postwar Italy. So they were not surprised when he asked if they would nominate him as a migrant.

By 1952 Giuseppe Varone had saved two fares, and with his eldest son, Jerrado, was back in Hyden. Arthur Marsh had agreed

199

Giuseppe and Jerrado Varone after their arrival in Australia, 1952.

to give him employment for two years.

Three years later Giuseppe and Jerrado had saved six thousand pounds, working as sleeper cutters and on the railways. Now, cash in hand, they were ready to become farmers themselves.

> *I went to see Arthur Marsh and he gave me a map with a block of land marked out.*
>
> *'This block's free, this block is free, this other block's free. Which one do you like best? Go and have a look and walk over it!'*
>
> *And so we did and we saw which one was the best. And so I bought two blocks, one for me and one for my son.*

It was a time of great opportunity for new settlers in the district. The Varones put themselves up in a tent, bought a tractor, cleared their first acreage and harvested it.

Jerrado took to Australia immediately. At times, however, he proved a worry to his father. On occasions when Giuseppe took a break by the woodheap to light a cigarette, Jerrado, exploiting his father's horror of snakes and reptiles in general, would throw his hands in the air and shout in mock terror, 'Goanne! Goanne!' The effect was immediate and gratifying.

All this time they had also been sending money home to Mrs Varone in Italy. The hard work paid off. Their fortunes improved with each successive clearing and fresh harvest.

By 1958 the family — Giuseppe, Filomena and remaining sons, Gino and Mario — were reunited for the second time, after another six-year separation. But this time they were to meet in Western Australia.

A neighbour and pioneer farmer of the Hyden district, Mick Mouritz, watched their progress with interest.

> *I never had a very high opinion of the land they had taken up. I'd seen one or two people have a go down there in that belt of country and they hadn't done well.*

I'd always held the opinion that it wasn't much good.
Anyway, it wasn't long before I had to change my mind
because the Varones came there as very hard-working
people and they developed the land, they worked hard,
they cut down a lot of country with axes and they've
grown a lot of crops, and I always feel they were very
welcome settlers in the district.

Today the Varone family, Joe, his wife, three sons and their
families, farm a combined total of twenty-nine thousand two
hundred acres.

Farmer's wife, Irene Falconer never heard from her POWs, Carlo
and Giuseppe (Joseph).

No, we never heard. I heard once from Joseph's brother
who was a doctor. He had a brother who was a doctor, a
brother who was a priest, and a sister who was an opera
singer. His brother wrote to thank us for being so kind to
his brother, but other than that, no, we never heard a
word. Carlos, the little one, always said he'd die of a
heart attack when he saw his mother. It would be too
much and he'd die. Well, whether he did or not I don't
know, because occasionally here in Australia, he would
be ill, and my husband took him into the doctor and he
said, yes, he did have a heart condition. If he wasn't a
worker we could send him back but if he worked we
could keep him. So we kept him. So whether he did have
a heart attack, I don't know, but we never heard a word,
not a word.

We were very sad about that. It seemed in a way
that all we had done was for nothing. But then we
tried not to think of it that way, we tried to think that
the excitement of going back home overcame everything
else.

Young Australians had left their homes during those war years. They had been sent to campaign in the Middle East but their war had ended in Europe. Now they, too, were coming home.

Jack Nelson, who had met his old playmate Tommy Della Bosca while on the run in Italy, survived imprisonment in Germany and returned to Katanning after the war. He was killed in 1949 by a falling tree while clearing land in the Great Southern district.

When Doug Le-Fevre came back to Australia he left the army and worked in a flour mill at Cottesloe. The job was hard and Doug found he was doing extra work on Saturdays to make up for some of his mates who were absent during the week. He soon decided to work for himself. The opportunity came when he and Eileen spotted a vacant property at Bullcreek. In 1947 they started a small poultry farm in countryside that now borders one of Perth's fast highways and is surrounded by suburbia. Eileen tells how Doug became known as 'The Duck King'.

> *The ducks and drakes loved Doug. They all used to run to meet him at the fence. And when the drakes started scrapping with each other in the 'bachelor's quarters' he only had to wave his broom handle or bang it down sharply on the verandah and they'd stop.*

Five years later they bought a trucking business to supply the building industry with bricks and sand. Doug named the new project 'Alberta Contractors', romantically celebrating Eileen's middle name. The proposition proved less romantic. The hours were long and the money they were owed often took a long time to come in. Their own costs were also high. Eileen remembers one day when every one of their seven trucks was off the road needing repair. Suddenly it seemed easier to sell houses than cart the raw materials to build them. Doug and Eileen went into real estate as partners for the next twenty-six years.

They visited Italy once after the war, on a crowded bus tour, passing briefly through Udine where Doug had been a prisoner of war. He could scarcely recognise the place.

Almost the first thing Jack Dodd did when he got back to Australia was to renew his prewar love of dancing. There was plenty of opportunity. At last the war was going in the Allies' favour, and although he was on stand-by for overseas service, he spent the rest of his military service in Western Australia. Whether in a holding camp at Melville or doing guard duty at Fremantle, Jack managed to get to a dance almost every night for a month, and met his wife-to-be, Vivienne, in the process.

He was keen to get out of the army, when the chance came. Life as a soldier had taught him much and, he reckons, its discipline probably saved his life more than once. But now:

> I wanted to lift that yoke and do something for myself.
> Mind you, some found it hard to leave the Army. They
> got used to being told what to do and some couldn't get
> on without that.

Jack himself took to his original life on the land, doing seasonal work, hay carting and, incidentally, carting the last loads of flax grown at Boyup Brook. He and Vivienne went into catering as well as farming, buying the Busselton tearooms and, later, taking up a farming property overlooking Geographe Bay near Dunsborough. The Dodds have two children and six grandchildren and see a great deal of them.

Jack has not been back to Italy nor spoken much of his extraordinary wartime experience.

> No, not much. People didn't ask much. As a matter of
> fact talking about it like this is probably the most I've
> ever spoken about it since I've been home.

But he has never forgotten the courage and kindness of the

Italian peasant families and partisans who helped them lie low, fed and sheltered them and organised their escape, sometimes at great risk to themselves and their own families. For Jack Dodd, they were generous to a fault.

> There were times there in Italy when I thought, 'These people have a wonderful heart.' We went to a place one night – they'd invited us to a meal – there were four of us POWs. And these people who'd invited us – they had nothing to eat. They gave us a plate of soup and it was just water with a bit of salt in it. They said that was all they had, and we felt dreadful taking it. But we honoured them and sat down and had a plate of soup with them. However, we were able to leave them a lot of other supplies because by that time we were heading towards Switzerland.

Jack Wauhop had seen enough of poverty in his own childhood in Fremantle to know it when he saw it. In East Fremantle fellow classmates came to school carrying wrapped lunches, food which they often offered excuses for not eating. One day, as if to prove he wasn't really hungry, a friend threw his lunch away. It hit the school playground with a dull clunk. The wrapping fell away and a block of wood rolled out.

Jack saw rural deprivation in Italy, too, but he also saw closeness and strong family support. He had survived, not only by his wits, but also through the generosity of strangers in a strange country.

In 1940 he had gone to war believing that Hitler and Mussolini had to be stopped. Six years later, with the war over, he wanted to put military life firmly behind him. In all that time what he had valued most was the behind the scenes work of both the Red Cross and the Salvation Army. For him they had been lifelines, providing channels of communication and much appreciated parcels in the POW camps where he had spent too much time. When he finally left his own army, 'There was no real thank you, no reward for your effort. You're just a number!'

For years afterwards it was difficult to talk about his experiences as both soldier and prisoner. Now he believes that the war

> ... took the violence out of me. You think of it now as a sheer waste of life. But at the time you're trained to kill and you do your best. At the time it all looked so threatening. All my mates had joined up. Two of my mates from school joined up the same day. We'll soon clean them up we thought.

And today?

> I'd go again if it was necessary; but just to volunteer, well, I'd look the other way.

Jack was never able to return to the farming work he had done before the war. His injuries at Gruppignano had seen to that. He could no longer hump bags of wheat or shift heavy hay bales. For some years after the war he worked for the Department of Works, driving bulldozers, clearing land and scooping out dams in the heavily timbered South-West of Western Australia. Later, as a result of that experience, he was able to set up his own trucking business.

Jack Hawkes arrived home on 15 August, VE Day 1945 via the Panama Canal, New Zealand and Sydney. He had travelled around the world on two shillings a day. The last time he had seen his wife, Joyce, was in a blur of speed at Claremont station, travelling non-stop for Fremantle and embarkation. That had been four years earlier. Now they were to meet at the same station. Once again he was coming in from Northam Army Camp. But this time the train stopped. Also there to meet him was the daughter he hadn't seen, born during the siege of Tobruk. She was now four and a half. Jack recalls that she didn't take to him on first acquaintance. Three more children were born in the 1950s.

Seeking a change of occupation, he applied through the postwar employment scheme for work in the timber industry but was told, 'You've got a job already!' He took up his former role as cinema projectionist for the next three years. In 1948 Jack joined Telecom as an Assistant Technician and worked in the communications industry for the next twenty-eight years.

He has not been back to Italy or revisited the scenes of his imprisonment in Austria, and wanted nothing more to do with the army or war. Four years of separation had made Jack Hawkes particularly appreciative of home life. He saw 'dreadful things' in that time but reckons he coped by trying to think of the whole experience as an adventure, and one which he was lucky to survive.

Dan Black was discharged in July 1945 and went back to Collie where he soon earned a reputation as a pugilist, a situation which the local police sergeant, Joe Ryan, sought to tame by suggesting that he join the police force. At the time Dan had gone back to work underground in the mine, but with his big frame was finding the job less than congenial and far from comfortable. Dan stayed in the police force for two years and then took on a variety of jobs, driving a cab and later carting superphosphate and grain through much of the Wheatbelt. He then moved interstate. For twenty-four years, between 1957 and 1981, he ran the Centennial Hotel in Woollahra, Sydney, before retiring to Perth.

He has revisited northern Italy three times and renewed wartime friendships among the partisans of the *Arditi* Squad. It was the men of the *Arditi*, incidentally, who captured Benito Mussolini, his entourage and much, Dan speculates, of his store of fine wine.

When he inspected a former partisan comrade's well-stocked cellar, some twenty years later, Dan regretted missing that moment in history. He had left the squad some time earlier.

There was another sequel to his time in Italy. When Dan Black met his former partisan comrade, Giouo, again, during that visit, he recalled his moment of disillusion with the partisans in 1944.

I said to him, 'Remember the night that you and the team shot those people outside the graveyard?' He said, 'No, it wasn't me, Dan.' I said, 'It was you. My memory is not that bad.' He said, 'No, it wasn't me.' I said, 'Oh yes it was.' He was really convincing. Anyway the following day we were coming back from the town of Polenya, where he lived. I was driving three hundred yards up this road and we passed the very graveyard where this all happened. I stopped the car. I said, 'Giouo, here's the gate of the graveyard and you were here.' He said, 'Danielli, Danielli, this is my village.' He said, 'I've got to live here. Please, please don't mention a word of it.' I said, 'All right, Giouo. I know what your position is. I won't say a word. But what about the two kids, what happened to them?' He said, 'They're in the village, they're all right.' So I let it go.

When Jim McMahon presented himself for demobilisation in the autumn of 1944 at Swanbourne Barracks, he chatted briefly with a contingent of Italian POWs, who had just been sent to Australia. From his speech they took him for an Italian. They were about to work in his country. In a way he'd been fighting for theirs. The British and Australian governments had just awarded him the Star of Italy medal in recognition of his work with the partisans.

Jim returned to the open-air life he'd lived before the war, working first at welding in Perth, and then at Yalgoo in the Murchison mining gold. Later he went further north again, this time back to the station at Carnavon where he had worked before the war. He set up and ran a banana plantation with a partner, supplementing this income by sinking wells and packing bananas for other plantation owners. He was much in demand on sheep stations as a goat shooter at eight shillings a skin. Jim prided himself on being able to skin a goat in forty-five seconds in those

Australian Military Forces

Certificate of Discharge

Certificate № 108834

This is to Certify that

------------------WX4445 Private Ronald James McMAHON---------------

---------------------2/28 Australian Infantry Battalion-------------

who enlisted for the-------- AIF --------on the 13 day of July 1940

and who Served on Continuous Full Time War Service

in the-------------------Australian Imperial Force--------------------

for a Total Effective Period* of ....

------------------One thousand five hundred & seventy nine---- Days

which included Active Service

In Australia† for-------59----days

Outside Australia† for---1346-- days

is Discharged from---------- Australian Imperial Force--------

During that service, or by virtue of that service, the
soldier was awarded, or became eligible for

Medals and Decorations   War Badge

....   Returned from Active Service
.........--------------.............   ----------A69682--------------
.........--------------.............

Major

Officer in Charge, ~~Records~~
WA ECHELON & RECORDS ~~Rxfxkxfxaxx~~

This Discharge takes effect on and from the Seventh
-----day of.....Nov.....One thousand nine hundred and forty.....four.....

Place.....Perth.....W.A.
Date.....9 Nov 44.......   for Confirming Authority.
         O.C. Discharge Company Western Command R.R. & G.D.

*"EFFECTIVE PERIOD" MEANS THE PERIOD OF SERVICE, LESS ANY CONSECUTIVE 21 DAYS OR MORE FOR WHICH THE SOLDIER WAS NOT ENTITLED TO PAY.
† "AUSTRALIA" MEANS THE MAINLAND OF AUSTRALIA AND TASMANIA.

Jim McMahon's Certificate of Discharge.

days. Later he married a girlfriend from Albany and had three daughters.

He has never been back to Italy and has never heard from any of the partisans or from his Scots pal, Tom Kelly, companion during his eventful months in Italy. They had come through much together. Both were Catholic and had attended mass together in many Italian churches during their partisan campaign. Somehow there had never been time to exchange addresses.

Phil Loffman returned to his old job, window-dressing at Frank Boans' store in Wellington Street, Perth. He worked there, as a Display Controller, for another forty-two years and was responsible for two spectacular celebratory displays; for the Queen's Coronation in 1953 and the Commonwealth Games in Perth in 1962. He also continued military service with the CMF, retiring as a captain in 1967.

In the last few years he has thought more and more about his time as a POW in Italy and later in German work camps. He is energetically collecting stories from the survivors of his own battalion and publishing them as fast as he can. He wants future generations to know that:

> *War is a madness. There's no logical sequence to the damage that is done because one party wants its way over another. I don't know what would have happened if they'd have won the war. I wouldn't be alive now, I can assure you of that. The life we were leading as slave labourers, I don't think we'd have got past fifty, and I don't think they'd have cared a damn.*

John Peck today lives quietly in retirement in Britian. His work, his experience and the networks he had built up were to prove of enormous help to Allied Intelligence in the remaining months of the war and in the postwar period. Later the Australian government awarded 'Captain' Peck, the Distinguished Conduct Medal

Top: Aldo Marogna, a former guard, at the site of Prisoner of War Camp PG57, Udine, Italy.
Bottom: The church at Camp PG57, Udine, Italy, which was entirely built by prisoners and is the only remaining structure from the camp.

211

but he was still a lieutenant in the Australian army when he led the Victorian contingent in the VE day parade in London in 1946. He returned briefly to Australia after hostilities ended, and was officially discharged from the army in 1946. He had had his fill of war. By 1947 Peck was back in Italy, this time as a genuine businessman, selling Australian exports to postwar Italy. Wartime contacts with the partisans still proved useful in peacetime

He had already married an English wife, in early 1945, and finally settled in England where he worked for over twenty-five years for the engineering and aircraft firm English Electric, which among its many products, built the Canberra bomber. His natural gift for languages, which had served him so well in the war, ensured that before long he became responsible for overseas sales and contracts. In 1972 Peck set up his own translation company for foreign language services. The company is still running although Peck himself has retired.

In the years immediately after the war he thought several times about returning to Australia, but somehow there was always another member of the family on the way. However, he has returned many times to Italy to meet his former comrades among the Italian partisans.

> *Yes, I've been back a number of times. Unfortunately quite a few of the people involved in the Luino disaster were executed, or were killed in concentration camps such as Dachau, Mitels and Belsen. Some were executed at Fossali concentration camp – that was in Italy. But of the remainder, I've seen them all as far as I could, and they lived ordinary lives until the time came and they died. A lot of them died early because of the privations of concentration camps or because of wounds suffered in those places, and I was surprised to find that the wives and children of the people who died didn't hold this against me at all. Incredibly, their greatness of heart was shown by the fact that for the man who betrayed us in*

Luino, they showed the utmost compassionate sympathy with his position.

As far as they were concerned, it was either see his parents tortured and murdered in front of him or betray his comrades. They rightly thought he did the correct thing in betraying his comrades rather than have his parents killed. They understood this through their emotionalism and their way of being so sympathetic to people in a predicament they couldn't get out of and not of their own making.

His name appears on the war memorials in the town together with the people he caused to be executed. Now I find that an amazing, and a heart-warming fact. But in the early days of my return there, I was most emphatically against it and I tried to have it changed, but bit by bit I've appreciated that he, too, had been a very brave man, had fought very well when he had to, and in his own judgement did the right thing and so I accept that.

John Peck's work for Allied prisoners of war is perhaps less well known than it should be. Settled in England, after the war, he bought a house in Stafford. The name he put on the door was San Vittore, the gaol in Milan where he had awaited execution in 1944. It was a reminder of luck as well as mortality.

PICTORIAL REFERENCES

Every effort has been made to locate copyright owners and to seek permission to reproduce images included in this book. The publisher would appreciate advice of copyright ownership in the cases where efforts have not been successful.

P12	Australian War Memorial, ref. 030239/9.
P16	Battye Library, ref. 4257B.
P20	Izzy Orloff. Battye Library.
P26	Australian War Memorial, ref. 064803.
P30	Abbondanza Vadala.
P35	Josephine Cabassi and Loretta Baldassar.
P37	Mary Fedele.
P41	Josephine Cabassi and Loretta Baldassar.
P43	Australian War Memorial, ref. 030239/44.
P48	Josephine Cabassi and Loretta Baldassar.
P50	Ben and Yvonne Mouritz.
P53	Phil Loffman.
P56	Pasquale Amato.
P58	Pasquale Amato.
P61	Lalage Falconer.
P64	Varone family.
P68	Prudence Broad.
P80	Smith family.
P84	Arthur Moore.
P89	Daily News.
P90	Phil Loffman.
P93	Phil Loffman.

P95	Phil Loffman.
P97	Phil Loffman.
P112	Phil Loffman.
P119	Phil Loffman.
P122	Phil Loffman.
P124	Margaret Ward.
P128	John Peck.
P136	Mrs Le-Fevre.
P141	Mrs Le-Fevre.
P142	Mrs Le-Fevre.
P153	Margaret Ward.
P156	John Peck.
P158	John Peck.
P168	John Peck.
P177	Phil Loffman.
P183	John Peck.
P184	Pasquale Amato
P190	Shire of Harvey.
P195	Anna Paolucci.
P198	Anna Paolucci.
P200	Varone family.
P209	Muriel McMahon.
P211	John Peck.